FIRST STEPS IN FAITH FOR NEW CHRISTIANS

by
CLAYTON PEPPER

Previously published as
BASIC BIBLE STUDIES FOR
CHRISTIAN GROWTH
by Maurice Tisdel.
Revised by Clayton Pepper

CONTENTS

chapter	title	page
1	First Steps In Faith	3
2	The Bible	5
3	How To Read The Bible	9
4	A New Life In Christ	15
5	Prayer	18
6	The Lord's Supper	21
7	You And Your Money	25
8	Church Attendance	29
9	The Indewelling Spirit	35
10	The Second Coming of Christ	42
11	The Church of Christ Is Scripturally Authentic	46
12	Finding My Place In The Church	52
13	Going On Unto Perfection	61

QUALITY PUBLICATIONS
P.O. BOX 7385
FT. WORTH, TEXAS 76111

TIPS FOR STUDENT AND TEACHER

TEACHER

This course is designed for edification of new Christians and the strengthening of others. It is ideal for teenagers in the classroom situation.

This course may be taught in a group or individually, at the church building or in a home.

All scripture references should be looked up and thoroughly explained in class. The lesson from the charts should be fully covered at this point in the lesson. The charts were prepared by Maurice Tisdel.

Some lessons are longer than others. If you complete a lesson before one class period is over, continue with the next lesson.

All blanks should be filled out by the student at home before coming to class.

Some congregations keep a New Christian's Class going at all times. When the student completes the thirteen lessons, he is promoted to another class.

STUDENT

Developing study habits requires much self discipline. It is easy to allow less important things to take all of our time. The following should be done in this course of study which is designed to help you become what God would have you be:

1. Study each lesson well before class.
2. Look up all scripture references. Make a list of questions that you have if you do not understand the scripture and discuss these questions in class.
3. Study the chart lesson.
4. Fill in the blanks after having read the scripture references.

Secure books that can help you answer others questions about your faith and strengthen your understanding of the Bible. The following will be helpful.

1. *Why I Am A Member Of The Church Of Christ,* by Leroy Brownlow.
2. *Nichol's Pocket Bible Encyclopedia,* by C. R. Nichols.
3. Subscribe to periodicals such as, *"The World Evangelist", "Personal Evangelism Magazine", Christian Family Magazine"* "Christian Bible Teacher Magazine" and "Power For Today".
4. *You Can Do Personal Work,* by Otis Gatewood.

Never quit reading your Bible and helpful books. If you do, you will die spiritually. May God bless you in your pursuit of the greatest life on earth!

First Steps In Faith

1

SCRIPTURE TEXT: "Blessed are they that hunger and thirst after righteousness: for they shall be filled." [*Matthew 5:6*].

INTRODUCTION

Becoming a Christian might be compared to a first grader starting to school. It is an entirely new world, with new friends and new responsibilities. There are many adjustments to make. There is no turning back, the price of little or no education is too high, the price must be paid.

For the new Christian who is not accustomed to going to church services regularly, it will require some changes in habits, schedules and family activities. Because of some adults being out of school for many years it will require some self discipline in order to become a student again; reading, studying and learning God's will for his life. Jesus said to His Apostles, "Go and make disciples." The word disciple means to discipline. This means all that goes into bringing us from a carnal, fleshly minded person who did not seek God first, to being a spiritually minded person who lives righteously and Godly in this present world. [*Titus 2:12*]. It would be a mistake to be concerned about being saved, but fail to see the many changes that must be made in our lives over a period of time in order that we may live a life pleasing to God.

Just as the child who starts to school will one day become productive in life, babes in Christ are to grow and become productive for Christ. Jesus said, "Freely ye have received, freely give." [*Matthew 10:8*]. Since we are already physically mature enough to be productive, there are many things that new Christians can do immediately. As they grow spiritually, they can do greater things for the cause of Christ.

First Steps In Faith

MAKE DISCIPLES **BAPTIZE** **TEACH**

1. Without faith we cannot please God. (Hebrews 11:6).
2. Faith is being sure about the things hoped for and certain about the things not seen. (Hebrews 11:1).
3. Faith comes from hearing and studying the Word of God. (Romans 10:17).
4. First steps in faith are based upon faith in Jesus as the Son of God. (John 8:24).
5. This faith led to the new birth — being born of water and the spirit. (John 3:3-5; Mark 16:16; Acts 2:38; 22:16).
6. When one has been born again, he is a new creature and a member of Christ's church. (II Corinthians 5:17; I Corinthians 12:13; Ephesians 1:22, 23).
7. The faith that leads one to obey the gospel must be increased. (II Peter 1:5-11; I Peter 2:2).

EXAMPLES OF FAITH

1. Abel showed faith in that he did not substitute his opinion for what God said. (Hebrews 11:4).
2. Enoch walked with God 300 years. By faith he pleased God. (Hebrews 11:5; Genesis 5:22).
3. Abraham's faith caused him to obey God's command to leave his homeland and go where God led him. His faith was tried when God told him to offer his only son as a sacrifice. (Hebrews 11:8-10, 17-19).
4. The faith of Israel produced obedience to God's command to march around the walls of Jericho seven days and the walls would fall down. (Joshua 6:12-15, 16 20; Hebrews 11:30).
5. Faith must be kept until death. (Revelation 2:10; Matthew 10:22; II Timothy 4:6-8).

FILL IN THE BLANKS

1. Is Christian growth a duty? What does Peter say about this? [*II Peter 3:18*]. ______________________

____

2. What are some of the things that one must put away in order to grow? [*I Peter 2:1*]. ______________________

____

3. What spiritual food does one need in order to grow? [*I Peter 2:2*]. ______________________

____

4. How can our friends affect our spiritual life? [*I Corinthians 15:33*]. ______________________

5. What did the new Christians in the Jerusalem church do to grow? [*Acts 2:42*]. ______________________

____

6. What happened to the Hebrew Christians who did not grow? [*Hebrews 5:11-14*]. ______________________

____

7. What was one of the problems of the Hebrew Christians? [*Hebrews 10:24-26*]. ______________________

____

8. How does spiritual growth cause us to be able to live in a mature manner? [*I Corinthians 13:11*]. ____________

____

9. Jesus describes four kinds of hearers, which one was pleasing to God? [*Matthew 13:23*]. ______________

____

10. When a Christian sins, how does he get forgiveness? [*I John 1:9*]. ________________________

____

Read Acts 8:10-24; James 5:16; Revelation 2:4; 5, 3:20.

The Bible

2

SCRIPTURE TEXT: "Every scripture inspired of God is also profitable for teaching, for reproof, for correction, for instruction which is in righteousness that the man of God may be complete, furnished completely unto every good work." [*II Timothy 3:16-17*].

INTRODUCTION

The Bible is a library of sixty-six books — thirty-nine in the Old Testament and twenty-seven in the New Testament. The Old Testament was written in the Hebrew language and began with the story of creation approximately 4,000 years B.C. (before Christ). The New Testament books were originally written in the Greek language. By the end of the first century A.D. (since Christ) the New Testament was completed.

The Bible was written by 40 different writers over a period of 1500 years. These men lived in different periods of history, followed different occupations and labored under different customs, governments and in different geographical locations. This was not humanly planned, co-ordinated and achieved. Yet, when put together in one great volume there is harmony and continuity of thought from the beginning to the end. This did not accidently occur! It came from God!

THE BIBLE

66 Books	40 Writers	1500 Years In Writing	4000 Years of History

THE OLD TESTAMENT

Law
Genesis
Exodus
Leviticus
Numbers
Deuteronomy

Poetry
Job
Psalms
Proverbs
Ecclesiastes
Song of Solomon

History
Joshua
Judges
Ruth
I Samuel
II Samuel
I Kings
II Kings
I Chronicles
II Chronicles
Ezra
Nehemiah
Esther

Prophets
Isaiah
Jeremiah
Lamentations
Ezekiel
Daniel

Minor Prophets
Hosea
Joel
Amos
Obadiah
Jonah
Micah
Nahum
Habakkuk
Zephaniah
Haggai
Zechariah
Malachi

THE NEW TESTAMENT

Biography
Matthew
Mark
Luke
John

History
Acts of the Apostles

Letters
Romans
I Corinthians
II Corinthians
Galatians
Ephesians
Philippians
Colossians
I Thessalonians
II Thessalonians
I Timothy
II Timothy
Titus
Philemon
Hebrews
James
I Peter
II Peter
I John
II John
III John
Jude

Prophecy
Revelation

THE BIBLE IS INSPIRED

Peter wrote, "For no prophecy ever came by the will of man: but men spake from God, being moved by the Holy Spirit." [*II Peter 1:21*]. God spoke in Old Testament times through the prophets, but now through His Son. "God, having of old time spoken unto the fathers in the prophets by divers portions and in divers manners, hath at the end of these days spoken unto us in his Son..." [*Heb. 1:1, 2*]. Jesus taught, selected and trained certain men to be His Apostles. He told them that he would be returning to His Father in Heaven and He would send the Holy Spirit to guide them. "But ye shall receive power, when the Holy Spirit is come upon you: and ye shall be my witness both in Jerusalem and in all Judea and Samaria and unto the uttermost part of the earth." [*Acts 1:8*]. After Jesus ascended to Heaven, the Holy Spirit came upon the Apostles. "And when the day of Pentecost was now come, they were all together in one place. And suddenly there came from heaven a sound as of the rushing of a mighty wind, and it filled all the house where they were sitting. And there appeared unto them tongues parting asunder, like as of fire; and it sat upon each one of them. And they were all filled with the Holy Spirit, and began to speak with other tongues, as the Spirit gave them utterance." [*Acts 2:1-4*]. While God's will was being revealed to man, the Apostles, along with certain others whom the Apostles had laid their hands on, were able to perform miracles to confirm that which they were teaching was from God. [*Mark 16:15-19*]. The last period of time began with Christ's resurrection from the grave. God's full revelation was made to man and spiritual gifts ceased. [*I Corinthians 13:8-13*]. Paul wrote that the scripture thoroughly furnishes us unto all good works. [*II Timothy 3:16-17; cf. Jude 3*]. The Old Testament testifies to the events recorded in the New Testament and the New Testament testifies to the Old Testament. But there is no reference to future revelations and dispensations. God's full revelation to man has been made. The Bible is the only book from God. It contains all that pertains to life and godliness. Man must not add to or take from its contents. [*Revelation 22:18, 19*].

GOD SPEAKS THROUGH THE BIBLE TODAY

God has revealed Himself to us through nature, but His complete revelation is only through the Bible. We come to know Him through His creation as Creator, but only through the Bible can we know Him as Father. The Bible is the only book that throws light on the past and future eternity, the realm of the otherwise unknown. Were it not for this light how great darkness would be! The Bible is revelation. Man longs to know from whence he came, why he is here, the state in which he is and where he is going. The Bible, as a revelation from God, tells man who his creator is, what God's purpose is for him and what his future will be. Things hidden are brought to light through this revelation from God. The obscure is made plain. Human knowledge cannot do this. We would be like the Indian of old, who expected a happy hunting ground beyond the grave, if it were not for the Bible. God's revelation of Himself has been gradual. The Patriarchal Age has been called the Star-light Age, the Mosacial Age, the Moonlight Age and the Christian Age the Sunlight Age. Things that were obscure to those before us are made plain. The Bible is Truth. Jesus said, "Sanctify them through thy truth." [*John 17:17*], "And ye shall know the truth and the truth shall make you free." [*John 8:32*]. Therefore, the word of God must be recognized as the only source of authority in matters of religion.

VERSIONS OF THE BIBLE

In recent years many versions of the Bible have appeared on the market. Paraphrase versions have proven to be a very profitable commercial enterprise. Such versions as *Good News For Modern Man, Living Bible, Philips Translation* and others like them, are not safe authorative translations of the scripture. When a group of scholars work toward translating the Hebrew of the Old Testament into today's English and the Greek of the New Testament into today's English, it is much more authoritative and reliable than a one man paraphrase version.

Many of these are really perversions of the scripture. Some of our best Bible scholars believe that the Revised and American Standard Versions are the most reliable. The International Edition is considered one of the most reliable new versions.

We suggest that you purchase a reliable version of the Bible, a Bible dictionary and concordance. A complete set of Bible commentaries should eventually be a part of your library. These can be purchased on the one-a-month plan at your bookstore. These will be mailed in the order that you desire and you will be billed each month. Set aside time to study God's Word regularly.

FILL IN THE BLANKS

1. How does study of the Bible enable one to be approved of God? [*II Timothy 2:15*]. ______________________

____

2. Can a man trust in himself for direction? [*Jeremiah 10:23*].

____

3. What may happen to those who do not love the Truth? [*II Thessalonians 2:10,11*]. ______________________

____

4. How can one be a hearer of the Word, yet be deceived? [*James 1:22-24*]. ______________________

5. What five things do we receive from the inspired Word? [*II Timothy 3:16, 17*]. (1)______________ (2)______

(3)____________ (4)___________ (5)__________

6. What two kinds of spiritual food do we read about in the Bible? [*I Peter 2:1, 2; Hebrews 5:12-14*].

____

____

7. How does the Word of God light man's pathway? [*Psalm 119: 105*]. ______________________________

____

8. How can Bible study help to keep us from falling? [*Ephesians 4:14; I Peter 1:5-11*]. ____________________

____

9. How can we know the things that we will face at judgment? [*Revelation 20:12; John 12:48*].

____

____

10. How does Bible study help us do God's work? [*Mark 16:15; Philippians 1:16; I Peter 3:15*]. (1) ____________

(2) ____________________ (3) ____________

____

____

How To Read The Bible

3

SCRIPTURE TEXT: "Give diligence to present thyself approved unto God, a workman that needeth not to be ashamed, handling aright the word of truth." [*II Timothy 2:15*].

INTRODUCTION

Much of the confusion and division among religious people today can be traced to a failure to properly divide the scripture. Peter referred to those who used some of Paul's writings to their own destruction. He said, "As also in all his epistles, speaking in them of these things; in which are some things hard to be understood, which they that are unlearned and unstable wrest, as they do also the other scriptures, unto their own destruction." [*II Peter 3:16*]. The Scripture must therefore be properly divided and understood.

When one studies the Bible it should be kept in mind who is speaking, to whom he is speaking, in what dispensation of time he is speaking and for what purpose. Keep in mind that while the Scripture is the Word of God, it also contains in recorded conversations and histories of events, the words of others beside God, Christ and the Holy Spirit or inspired men. While the Word was written by inspired men, it quotes, even the words of the devil, or of evil misguided or misinformed men. Know something of what precedes and what follows that you may use it with the insight of the context. God's law of pardon for an erring Christian is not the same as for one who has not yet become a Christian.

Each scripture should be interpreted in the light of other scripture. Let the plain passages explain the obscure ones.

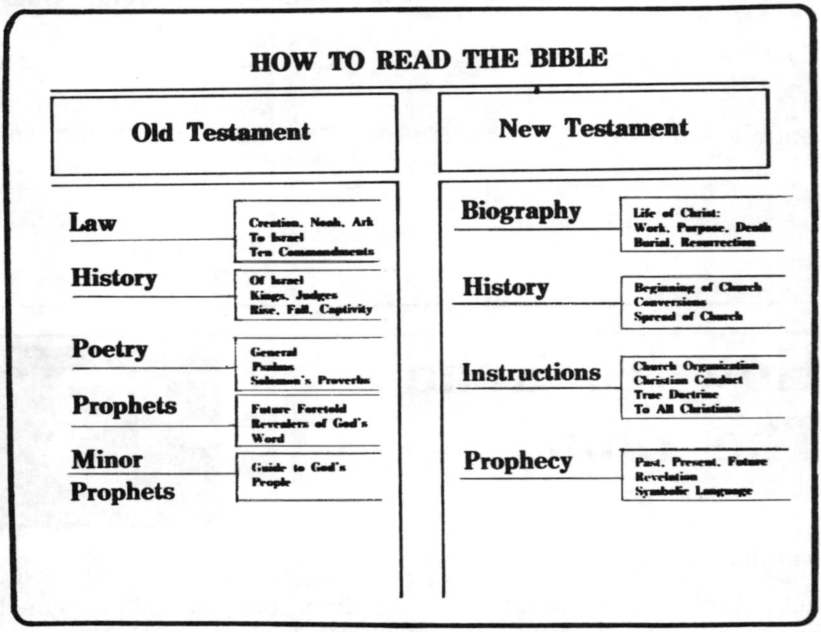

THE BIBLE CAN BE UNDERSTOOD

If the Bible could not be understood it would be worthless to us. Some have been taught that the average person cannot understand the Bible, but this is a contradiction of the Bible itself. Many passages indicate that we can understand. For instance, "Wherefore be ye not unwise, but understanding what the will of the Lord is." [*Ephesians 5:17*]. After all, why would God write a message to men that they could not understand and tell them in that message what He required of them? Why would Paul exhort Timothy to read and study if he could not understand? He said, "Study to show thyself approved unto God, a workman that needeth not to be ashamed, rightly dividing the word of truth." [*II Timothy 2:15*].

DIVISIONS OF THE BIBLE

Every book, magazine or lengthy article has its divisions. Even the newspapers are divided into sections which have special interests to different people. Some will be interested in the sports page, some in the editorials, and others in the want ads. Our history books include certain periods of time, but are divided so that a reader can fix his mind on certain people and events that make history. In this way things fall into some order which helps us to remember them.

So it is with the Bible. The sacred historians begin at the beginning of creation. The end of the Bible brings it to a close with a glimpse of the future in which we all ought to have a very real interest. The Scriptures indicate the absolute authority of God as He worked through prophets and apostles. He has spoken to us by the Word which was written to instruct us into a life of service and obedience, and eventually to have an entrance into Heaven granted us. The Bible is divided into about eight major divisions. Each one of these stands out very clearly and has a special purpose. Let us look at each of these divisions and we will see that the Bible is easier to understand by recognizing them.

PURPOSE OF THE OLD TESTAMENT

If we did not have the Old Testament we would not know how the worlds came to exist, the origin of man, the beginning of sin or why good and evil exists in the world. But in Romans 15:4 we find that "whatsoever things were written aforetime were written for our learning, that we through patience and comfort of the Scriptures might have hope." There are many examples in the Old Testament, both of good and evil, that are warnings to us. They show us the attitude of God toward sin. All through the Old Testament the writers point in various ways to the coming of Christ.

After telling about the deliverance of Israel from Egyptian bondage and about their great sins against God, and about their punishment, Paul says, "Now these things were our examples to the intent we should not lust after evil things, as they also lusted." [*I Corinthians 10:6*]. The 11th verse says, "Now all these things happened unto them by way of example; and they were written for our admonition, upon whom the ends of the ages are come."

DIVISIONS OF THE OLD TESTAMENT

(See chart for books in each sub-division).

The first five books of the Bible are usually called the Law. The book of Genesis comes to a close with the children of Israel in Egypt. Moses was appointed their leader, and under him they left Egypt and began their journey toward Canaan, the land that God had promised to them first through Abraham. But God gave a law to Moses for the people of Israel. [*Exodus 20*]. It was written upon tables of stone and in a book. This law was given only to Israel and lasted until Christ fulfilled it, took it out of the way, and gave the gospel as the "faith once for all delivered to the saints." [*Jude 3*]. Incidentally, we must remember that Jesus was born and died under the law. [*See Galatians 4:4-6; Colossians 2:14-17*].

The next twelve books are books of history. They begin with Joshua and end with Esther. It was in this period of time that Israel threw off the rule of God and demanded a king to rule over them as the other nations around them. In 722 B.C. the nation of Israel was taken into captivity by the Assyrians. And in 606 B.C. Judah was carried into captivity by the Babylonians. God had promised to send Christ to the people through the tribe of Judah, and for that reason he held them together and brought them back to their home land. Jesus was born of a woman in this tribe, but today no Jew could tell you from what tribe he has come.

The third section is a group of poetic works. They are Job, Psalms, Proverbs, Ecclesiastes and Song of Solomon. The books of Psalms and Proverbs are the best known of these. David had a lot to say about Christ and His Kingdom in the Psalms.

The fourth is composed of seventeen books of prophecy. They begin with Isaiah and end with Malachi. These prophets wrote of many things that had to do with the social and religious evils of the day. But they are much more important to us because they tell us much about Christ and the New Testament church that was to be established. Micah even tells us where the Christ was to be born. When we read prophecies and then turn to the Scriptures and find them fulfilled exactly as the prophets said we have greater faith in God because of their fulfillment. Men cannot foretell future events without God's help.

THE NEW TESTAMENT

(Refer to charts for books in each sub-division.)

The purpose of the entire New Testament is to produce faith in Christ as the Son of God, teach us how to become Christians, and how to live so that we will be saved eternally. These are divided into four sections, also.

There are four books which are records of the life of Christ. They are sometimes called the four Gospels. There is one verse that tells us why these books were written. It is in John

20:30-31. It says, "And many other signs truly did Jesus in the presence of His disciples, which are not written in this book: But THESE ARE WRITTEN THAT YE MIGHT BELIEVE THAT JESUS IS THE CHRIST; and that believing ye might have life in his name." You know, "Faith comes by hearing the Word of God." [*Romans 10:17*]. So what is written in the four "gospels" is to produce faith in our hearts, — faith in Jesus as God's Son.

The second section is Acts. The book of Acts is as important to us in understanding the New Testament as the book of Genesis is to the understanding of the whole book. It is in the Acts that we find the coming of the Holy Spirit upon the apostles to guide them in their preaching. In Acts 2 we have the first gospel sermon that was preached after Christ arose from the dead, and the first time that the Church is spoken of as actually being in existence. [*Acts 2:47*].

Then the history of the church of the first century follows. Peter is the chief character in the first part of Acts; Paul is the chief character in the latter half beginning with chapter thirteen.

The third section: The Church has been established; men and women have been taught how to BECOME CHRISTIANS. Then, of course, they must learn how to live as Christians. So the 21 epistles, or letters, that follow are for that purpose. A letter was written to a congregation or to an individual for a special purpose. Some letters are very general and were sent to all the churches. But in all of them the problems were dealt with that were prevalent in that day. In principle we have those same problems with us in every generation so that the Bible is perfect and complete for its intended purpose.

The last section, or division, is the Revelation. It is usually called a book of prophecy. The main purpose of Revelation is to show the final victory of the Church over the world, and the final victory of Christ over Satan. It is certainly intended that we should catch a glimpse of heaven and hell that we might be encouraged to be faithful to the Lord and be with Him forever in the everlasting kingdom. [*II Peter 1:5-11*].

Jesus said, "Search the Scriptures; for in them ye think ye have eternal life: and they are they which testify of me." [*John 5:39*]. Paul states that he would not have his brethren to be ignorant. Then he goes right on telling them what they should know and understand. We can also understand what the Lord wants us to know. Most everyone knows that the Bible is divided into the Old and New Testaments.

FILL IN THE BLANKS

1. What is the greatest book in the world?__________

2. Give two names for the Bible found within it.______

____

3. Into what two great divisions has the Bible been divided?

____

4. How many books are there in the Old Testament?____

How many books are there in the New Testament?___

5. Into what five groups may the Old Testament be divided? [*We only have four sections by grouping the major and minor prophets*].______________________________________.

6. How many books are there of Law?________Name them:____

7. How many books are there of History?__________

Name them:________________________________

8. How many books are there of Poetry?________Name them:____

9. How many books are there of Major Prophets?______

Name them:________________________________

10. How many books are there of Minor Prophets?____

Name them:________________________________

11. Into what four groups may the books of the New Testament be divided?______________________________

____

12. How many books are there of Biography?______

Name them:________________________________

13. How many books of History?________ Name it:____

14. How many books of special letters or Epistles?_____

Name them:________________________________

---

15. How many books of Revelation or Prophecy? ______

Name it: ____________________________

A New Life In Christ

4

SCRIPTURE TEXT: "Wherefore if any man is in Christ, he is a new creature: the old things are passed away: behold, they are become new." [*II Corinthians 5:17*].

INTRODUCTION

Paul beautifully expressed his devotion to Christ when he wrote, "I have been crucified with Christ; and it is no longer that I live, but Christ liveth in me: and that life which I now live in the flesh I live in faith, the faith which is in the Son of God, who loved me, and gave himself up for me." [*Galatians 2:20*]. The "old" Saul that had persecuted the church was now Paul who loved the church. He said, "Christ liveth in me . . ." Now that we are new creatures in Christ, we are no longer led by fleshly lusts and desires, but by the will of God. [*Galatians 5:16-25*].

A new life in Christ brings new relationships. God is our Father. [*Galatians 3:26, 27*]. Christ is our Saviour. [*Ephesians 5:23*]. We have brothers and sisters in Christ who strive for the good of each other. We are the body of Christ, the Church. [*Ephesians 5:30; 1:22, 23*]. Paul said, ". . . Christ also loved the Church, and gave himself up for it; that he might sanctify it, having cleansed it by the washing of water with the word, that he might present the Church to himself a glorious Church, not having spot or wrinkle or any such thing; but that it should be holy and without blemish. [*Ephesians 5:25-28*]. A new life in Christ means denying ourselves, ". . . ungodliness and worldly lusts, we should live soberly and righteously and godly in this present world; looking for the blessed hope and appearing of the glory of the great God and our Saviour Jesus Christ; who gave himself for us, that he might redeem us from all iniquity, and purify unto himself a people for his own possession, zealous of good works." [*Titus 2:12-14*].

A NEW LIFE IN CHRIST

A NEW LIFE REQUIRES A NEW BIRTH	Old Things	New Things	
	PASSED AWAY	REMAIN	
The Begettal			
Bringing Forth *I Pet. 1:23*	Leader.....Satan Works.....Evil Heart.....Impure Desires.....Unholy Serving.....Flesh	Leader.....Christ Works.....Good Heart.....Pure Desires.....Holy Serving.....God	**Relationship and Purpose** **God the Father of All** **Christ Head of the church** *I Cor. 11:3; Col. 1:18*
Spirit Begets *John 6:62; I Cor. 4:15*			
Baptism Brings Forth *Rom. 6:3, 4; Gal. 3:27*			
Born of Water & Spirit *John 3:5*	WORKS OF FLESH	FRUIT OF SPIRIT	LOCAL ARRANGEMENTS
Enter Into Kingdom	Adultery Fornication Uncleanness Idolatry	Love Joy Peace Longsuffering	Elders to oversee Deacons to serve Members to work *I Tim. 3:1-13; Matt. 25:14-30*
Enter Into Family	Hatred Wrath	Gentleness Goodness	PURPOSE
Enter Into Church	Strife Envying Murders	Faith Meekness	Separate from world Save ourselves — Obedience Save others — Evangelize Do will of the Father
Enter Into Christ *II Cor. 5:17; Col. 3:1; Acts 2:47*	Drunkenness Such-like	Temperance Against Such There Is No Law *Galatians 5:19-24*	Glorify God in heaven *II Cor. 6:14-17; Rom. 12:2; II Tim. 2:2; Matt. 5:16*

FILL IN THE BLANKS

1. A new life requires a new______________. [*John 3:5*].

2. There are two things necessary for the new birth. The ______________and the __________.[*John 3:5*].

3. The begettal power is the __________of ________. [*I Peter 1:23*].

4. The coming forth is from ______________. [*Romans 6:3, 4; Colossians 2:12*].

5. To be born of the water and the Spirit, [*John 3:5*]. one must be begotten by the ___________and be______ in water. This puts one into ________________. [*Galatians 3:27*].

6. If any man be in ___________he is a new creature. [*II Corinthians 5:17*].

7. God ______________us into the kingdom. [*Colossians 1:13, 14*].

8. God ___________the saved to the _________. [*Acts 2:47*].

9. We are __________ with ___________ to walk in newness of life. [*Colossians 3:1; Romans 6:4*].

10. There is no _______________ to them who are in Christ. [*Romans 8:1*].

11. There is now the assurance of ———————— ——————————————— if we remain faithful. [*I John 5:13*].

12. God will bless us with our physical needs if we ——————————————— him ———————————————. [*Matthew 6:33; Phillipians 4:19; Hebrews 13:5*].

13. God will answer our ————————————————. [*I John 5:14-15*].

14. All things will work for our ———————————as long as we ——————————————— him. [*Romans 8:28; Phillipians 2:13*].

15. We have ———————————— with God. [*Phillipians 4:6-7*].

16. We have ————————————from————————————in Christ. [*I Peter 5:6-7*].

OLD THINGS PASSED AWAY

1. Who is the God of this world? ——————————————— [*II Corinthians 4:4*].

2. Name five items of the works of the flesh. *Galatians 5:19-21*]. (1) ————————————————(2)—————————— (3)————————————(4)—————————————————— (5)——————————————————————————————.

3. How do we dispose of our evil desires and habits? [*Colossians 3:5*].——————————————————————————

4. Will we as children of God be free from temptation? —————————————————————————————.[*James 1:14*].

5. Do we have assurance that we can overcome temptation? [*I Corinthians 10:13*]. ——————————————————————

6. Is it a sin to be tempted? —————————When does it become a sin? [*James 1:12-15*].—————————————————

7. What are the conditions of forgiveness to a child of God when he does wrong? —————————————— and ———— ——————————————————God. [*Acts 8:22; I John 1:9*].

8. Can we be neutral in regard to the Lord's work?_____

__________________. [*Matthew 12:30*].

5 Prayer

SCRIPTURE TEXT: "Pray without ceasing; in everything give thanks: for this is the will of God in Christ Jesus to you-ward." [*I Thessalonians 5:17-18*].

INTRODUCTION

Prayer is a vital part of the Christian life. Those who obeyed the gospel the day the Church began continued steadfastly in prayer. [*Acts 2:42*]. Jesus' disciples said to Him on one occasion, ". . . teach us to pray, even as John also taught his disciples." [*Luke 11:1*]. We should also feel the need to learn to pray.

Why do people pray? Someone has said, "many people use God like a lawyer, the only time they call on Him is when they are in trouble." This is too often true. Should it take a crisis to cause us to pray or should being aware of God's goodness toward us daily, thus out of a heart of gratitude and thanksgiving, cause us to talk to God? ". . . but in everything by prayer and supplication with thanksgiving let your requests be made known unto God." [*I Thess. 5:18*]. Learn to count your blessings daily. Do not be a negative thinker who only sees the bad! You will never see your blessings. Learn to pray daily. Paul said, "pray without ceasing." We should always have an attitude of prayer. Talk to God while you work, while you drive, before you go to sleep, at the table giving thanks for food, in family devotionals, as well as in church services. (Subscribe for *Power For Today,* a family devotional guide. Send subscription to: 20th Century Christian, 2809 Granny White Pike, Nashville, Tennessee 37204).

Prayer should be addressed to God. It includes adoration, praise, thanksgiving, petitions or requests, and closes in Christ's name.

PRAYER

Why	How	Benefits
To Commune with God *Phil. 4:16*	In Christ's Name *John 14:13*	God Hears His Own *John 9:31*
To Receive Strength *Matt. 6:13*	In Faith *Matt 21:22; Jas. 1:6, 7*	Blesses Them *I Tim. 2:1, 2*
To Obtain Grace *Heb. 4:16*	By Will of God *II Thess. 5:17, 18*	Forgives Them *Matt. 6:12, 14, 15*
To Praise His Name *Matt. 6:9*	Doing God's Will *I John 5:14; Matt. 6:10*	Receives Strength *Matt. 6:13*
Seek Forgiveness *Matt. 6:12, 14, 15; James 5:16*	With Pure Heart *James 4:3*	Encouragement *Lk. 18:1*
Pray For Others *James 5:16; Matt. 6:12*	With Perseverance *Rom. 12:12; I Cor. 7:5; Eph. 6:18*	Gives Hope *James 5:16*
Spiritual Needs *Matt. 6:12; Acts 8:22; James 5:16*	With Forgiveness *Matt. 6:14, 15*	Be Remembered

FILL IN THE BLANKS

1. What request did the disciples make of Jesus? [*Luke 11:1*].

____

2. What will the prayer of a righteous man avail? [*James 5:16*]. ______________________________________

3. Underline the words that define prayer: beseech, proclaim, entreat, exalt, earnest request, condemn, supplication, sanctify.

4. What did James say to do for one another? [*James 5:16*].

____

5. Does prayer have anything to do with influencing God? [*Numbers 11:1, 2; I Samuel 12:16-18*]. ______________

6. In whose name should we pray? [*John 14:14*]. ________

7. In praying we should always ask in ______________ [*James 1:6, 7*].

8. Faith comes by ______________________. [*Romans 10:17*].

9. The answer to prayer would be limited to what is taught in God's Word. Yes __________________ No _____.

10. We should always pray according to the _________ of ______________________. [*I John 5:14*].

11. Does the answer to prayer depend on our doing the will of God? Yes------ No ------. [*I John 3:21, 22; John 9:31*].

12. What condition must my heart be in for God to hear my prayers?------------------------------.

13. Should I have a prayerful attitude at all times?------. [*I Thessalonians 5:17*].

14. Must I have forgiveness in my heart to expect God to forgive me?--------------------.[*Mark 11:25*].

15. When I pray should there be any doubt in my heart?--------------------[*I Timothy 2:8*].

16. He that turneth away his ear from hearing the --------- even his ----------shall be -----. [*Proverbs 28:9*].

17. Will God hear a sinner's prayer? ------------ [*John 9:31*].

18. What two requirements are given for acceptable prayer? [*John 9:31*].

(1) ----------------------------

(2) ----------------------------

19. Does it make any difference whether I stand, kneel or sit when I pray? ----------------[*Acts 20:36; Mark 11:25*].

20. Does the condition of mind depend on the posture of the body?----------------------------

The Lord's Supper

6

SCRIPTURE TEXT: "And as they were eating, Jesus took bread, and blessed, and brake it; and he gave to the disciples, and said, Take eat; this is my body. And he took a cup, and gave them, saying, Drink ye all of it; for this is my blood of the covenant, which is poured out for many unto remission of sins." [*Matthew 26:26-28*].

INTRODUCTION

In the Old Testament book of Exodus we read of the enslavement of the children of Israel in the land of Egypt under King Pharoah. He had refused to let them leave, as God had directed, under the leadership of Moses. God brought ten plagues upon the land before the King would give consent for them to leave. The last plague was the death of the eldest child in each family. However, God made special provisions for the children of Israel. They put the blood of a lamb on the lintel and two side posts of the door. The Lord saw the blood and passed over that house and the eldest in that family did not die. God did not want the adults or their children to forget this occasion. Therefore, God commanded that this passover be remembered and observed. "And it shall come to pass, when your children shall say unto you, What mean ye by this service? That ye shall say, It is the sacrifice of Jehovah's passover, who passed over the houses of the children of Israel in Egypt, when he smote the Egyptians, and delivered our houses. And the people bowed the head and worshipped. [*Exodus 12:26, 27*].

Jesus was eating the passover when He instituted a memorial to His own death to save the people from spiritual death. The unleavened bread represented His body. The cup was the fruit of the vine, representing His blood. [*I Cor. 11:25*]. Paul writes of the institution of the Lord's supper, adding that Jesus said, ". . . this do in rememberance of me." [*I Corinthians 11:24*]. The blood of a lamb saved many from death in Egypt. Jesus came as the ". . . Lamb of God that taketh away the sin of the world!" [*John 1:29*]. His death, burial and resurrection provided a way for man to escape spiritual death, the loss of the soul. Through our obedience to the gospel, we like Israel can rejoice because of deliverance. We too, are to remember our deliverance from sin, and the one whose blood made that deliverance possible, by observing the Lord's Supper.

THE LORD'S SUPPER

Matt. 26:26-29 — *I Cor. 11:23-29*

Animal Sacrifices	Death of Christ	The Lord's Supper
GOD'S PLAN *Genesis 4:3-5; Lev. 1:1-9* WITHOUT SPOT *Numbers 19:2; 28:3, 9; 29:17, 26* BLOOD SHED *Lev. 1:1-15* IN REMEMBRANCE OF SIN *Heb. 8:12; 10:17* BLOOD OFFERED *Lev. 1:5; 16:14-16* GOD PLEASED *Genesis 4:4-5; Heb. 11:4* OFFERED EACH YEAR *I Samuel 1:21; 2:19; Heb. 9:7, 25; 10:1-3*	GOD'S PLAN *Matt. 16:21; 26-39* WITHOUT SIN *I Peter 2:21-24; Matt. 27:24; Lk. 23:14* BLOOD SHED *Matt. 26:28* FOR REMISSION OF SINS *Heb. 9:22; Matt. 26:28* BLOOD OFFERED *John 19:34* GOD PLEASED *John 3:16; John 6:38* ONLY ONE OFFERING *Heb. 7:27; 10:12, 18*	CHRIST'S COMMAND *Matt. 26:26-29; Mark 14:22-24* BREAD & FRUIT OF VINE *Matt. 26:26-29* REPRESENTS CHRIST'S BODY AND BLOOD *I Cor. 11:24-26; Matt. 26:26-28* OBSERVE IN MEMORY *I Cor. 11:24* PARTAKE WORTHILY *I Cor. 11:27-30* REGULARLY *Acts 2:42; 20:7* ON FIRST DAY EACH WEEK *Acts 20:7*

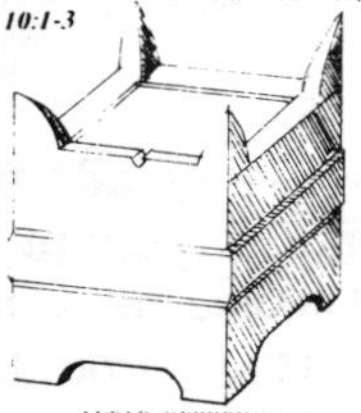

ALTAR OFFERING

CROSS OF CHRIST

LORD'S TABLE

FILL IN THE BLANKS

I. THE ATONEMENT IS THE CENTRAL FACT OF HISTORY AND HAS A PROMINENT PLACE IN THE TEACHINGS OF BOTH THE OLD AND NEW TESTAMENTS.

A. The animal sacrifices of the Old Testament are symbolic of great truths in the ________________________

1. The Jewish tabernacle was "a figure (type) for the ________________________[*Hebrews 9:1-5*].

2. The tabernacle, its furnishings and the high priest are called a figure? Yes_____ No _____. [*Heb. 9:1-10*].

3. It is said in the Hebrew letter that the law had "a __________________of good things to come", therefore, it can make perfect those that draw near to it. Yes.__________ No __________.[*Hebrews 10:1*].

B. Many of the ordinances of the ________________ pointed unmistakeably to the shedding of the _________ of Christ upon the cross.

1. The Altar of ——— ——————

pointed directly to the —————————death of Christ. [*Exodus 27:1-8; Numbers 28*]. The blood of the animal sacrifices

was——————————of the——————————-— death of Christ. [*Hebrews 9:11-28*].

2. The Passover, the —————————— of all Jewish

feasts, pointed once each year to the ———————— death

of Christ, the —————————— of God. [*Exodus 12:1-28; I Corinthians 5:7*].

3. "And according to the law, I may almost say, all things are cleansed with blood, and apart from shedding of blood there is no remission." [*Hebrews 9:22*]. "The next day John seeth Jesus coming unto him, and saith, Behold the ———————— of God, that taketh away the sin of the world." [*John 1:29*].

II. CHRIST THE DIVINE SON GOD PERSONALLY INSTITUTED THE LORD'S SUPPER BEFORE HIS CRUCIFIXION. [*Matthew 26:26-29; Mark 14:22-25*].

1. It is to be observed in ———————— of a divine

person ————————————————. [*Luke 22:19; I Corinthians 2:23-25*].

2. When Jesus instituted it He declared He would not eat

it again until He ate it anew with them in the—————————

———————————————————————. [*Matthew 26:29*].

3. Give two scriptures showing that the Lord's Supper became a part of the worship of the New Testament church:

(1). ——————————————————————————

(2). ——————————————————————————

4. Can there be any doubt that the early church practiced meeting regularly the first day of every week? Yes

———————— No ————————. [*Acts 20:7; I Corinthians 16:1-2; Acts 2:42; 20:7*].

a. —————————— typifies the death, burial and resurrection of Christ. [*Romans 6:3, 4*].

b. The ———————— —————————— memorializes the death of Christ on the Cross. [*I Corinthians 11:26*].

c. The Lord's Supper is not to be observed as a Love Feast, but done in rememberance of ——————————— [*I Corinthians 11:17-22*].

5. Do unsaved people have a right to this memorial table? Yes ————————————— No ———————————.

a. The ——————, as such, has no right to this table. [*Hebrews 13:10*].

b. This is the Lord's table, and only the ——————— people have a right to it. [*I Corinthians 10:21*].

6. In partaking of the Lord's Supper each one must ———————————————himself. [*I Corinthians 11:28*].

a. We should also examine our brother. Yes ————— No ———————.

7. In examining ourselves:

a. We should not come with ———————— in our hearts for anyone. [*John 2:9*].

b. We should not come with ——————————toward our brother, or with any ———————— ————————— against our brother upon our souls. [*Matthew 5:23-24*].

c. We should not come with a self-righteous spirit as the Pharisees, but in an humble spirit. [*I John 1:8, 9*].

d. We should observe the Lord's Supper every ————— —————————— ——————— ————————

e. It is the communion of the —————————and —————————— of the Lord. [*I Corinthians 10:16*].

f. It should be a time of ———————————————.

g. It is a —————————————— occasion. [*I Corinthians 11:26*].

You and Your Money

7

SCRIPTURE TEXT: "Upon the first day of the week let each one of you lay by him in store, as he may prosper, that no collection be made when I come." [*I Corinthians 16:2*].

INTRODUCTION

In every dispensation men have been taught to give or sacrifice to God; hence the giving of our means has always been a matter of concern to Him.

(1) In the early dawn of time, ". . . Cain brought of the fruit of the ground an offering unto Jehovah. And Abel, he also brought of the firstlings of his flock and of the fat thereof. And Jehovah had respect unto Abel and to his offering: but unto Cain and to his offering he had not respect. And Cain was very wroth and his countenance fell." God would not accept just any offering then and neither will He today. This should cause us to give serious thought to our giving.

(2) Jesus showed concern for the people's giving. "And He sat down over against the treasury, and beheld how the multitude cast money into the treasury . . ." [*Mark 12:41*]. Jesus was interested in what they gave and He is interested in what we give.

(3) The Lord was watching when Ananias and Sapphira made their gift. [*Acts 5:1-11*]. In a vain effort to receive the praise of men, they lied about their giving. They were executed for this evil deed. This brought fear upon the early church and taught a lesson that when one thinks he can deceive God, he only deceives himself. [*Galatians 6:7*].

From these foregoing examples we see that God is interested in our giving. It is another avenue whereby God blesses the faithful. If we sow bountifully we shall reap bountifully. If we sow sparingly, we shall reap sparingly. [*II Corinthians 9:6*].

How much should we give? Paul said, "As God hath prospered him." The amount we give is in proportion to what we receive. There is justice and fairness in God's command. Everyone, whether he makes little or much can obey it. "For if the readiness is there it is acceptable according as a man hath, not according as he hath not." [*II Corinthians 8:12*]. Under the inferior law of Moses they were to give a tenth. We have a better covenant based on better promises. [*Hebrews 8:6*]. We live in the most prosperous nation in the world. Jesus expected the righteousness of His disciples to exceed that of the scribes and Pharisees.

YOU AND YOUR MONEY

Examples	Commands	Purposes	Substitutes
Abraham *Gen. 22*	As we Prosper *I Cor. 16:2*	To Preach Gospel *I Cor. 9:13,14*	Taxing Members
His Son	As we Purpose	For the Poor Saints *Rom. 15:26*	Church Dinners
God *John 3:16*	Cheerfully *II Cor. 9:6, 7*	For the Needy	Rummage Sales
His Son	Liberally	To Bear Fruit *Phil. 4:15-19*	Pie Suppers
Early Christians	On First Day of Week	To Obey God *Rev. 22:14*	Shows
All Their Goods *Acts 4:34, 35*	Faithful to Stewardship	To Glorify God *Eph. 3:21*	Raffles
Gave Themselves			Entertainment
The Corinthians *II Cor. 8:5*			Assessment

FILL IN THE BLANKS

I. GOD'S CAUSE HAS ALWAYS DEPENDED IN A MEASURE ON MATERIAL THINGS.

The example, command and purpose of giving are made plain in the teachings of God's Word.

1. God gave man dominion over all the ————————— of the field, the ———————— of the air, and the ———————————— in the sea. [*Genesis 1:26*].

2. God gave man a beautiful home in the garden of ——————————————. [*Genesis 1:8*].

3. Everything man has belongs to ——————————————. [*I Corinthians 10:26*].

4. "We brought ————————— into the world, and it is certain we can carry ——————————out. And having ————————— and —————————— let us therewith be content." [*I Timothy 6:7-8*].

II. EXAMPLES OF GIVING TO THE LORD, AND BY THE LORD.

1. Abel gave the ——————— of the flock. [*Genesis 4:4*].

2. When the Jews made an offering, God required the ————————— of their flock. [*Deuteronomy 12:6*].

3. Abraham gave his ————————— as an offering. [*Genesis 22*].

4. God gave His ————————— ————————— ————————— for us.

5. The early church sold their —————————, and brought the —————————and laid it at the Apostles feet. [*Acts 4:37*].

5. The Corinthians first gave —————————unto the Lord. [*II Corinthians 8:5*].

III. GOD COMMANDS US TO GIVE OF OUR MATERIAL THINGS.

1. We are to give upon the ————————— day of the week. [*I Corinthians 16:2*].

2. Who is to give —————————. [*I Corinthians 16:2*].

3. Our giving is to be determined by how the Lord has ————————— us. [*I Corinthians 16:2*].

4. The elders are to teach us how much we should give. Yes —————— No ——————.

5. Every man according as ————————— in his heart, so let him give.

6. If we give ————————— we shall also reap —————————. [*II Corinthians 9:6*].

7. The Lord loves a —————————. [*II Corinthians 9:7*].

8. God holds us responsible for all that is in our possession. Yes —————— No ——————.

9. Does the Lord require anything unreasonable? —————————. [*Romans 12:1*].

10. To give liberally is to give according to what we have,

and not according to what someone else gives. A five dollar gift by one person might be a sacrifice, while with someone else it might be disobedience to God to give that little. Yes——————

No ——————.

IV. THE PURPOSE OF GIVING

1. To obey ———————————————. [*Hebrews 5:8-9*].

2. They that —————————— the gospel shall —————————— by the gospel. [*I Corinthians 9:14*].

3. The —————————— is the power of God unto salvation. [*Romans 1:16*].

4. The work of the Church depends upon our giving ——————————. [*II Corinthians 8:1*].

5. Liberal giving will not deprive us of the necessities of life. Yes —————— No ——————. [*II Corinthians 9:8*].

6. Poor saints, not only in our midst, but in other places are dependent upon our giving. Yes —————— No ——————. [*Romans 15:26*].

7. As we therefore have —————————— let us do good unto ———————————— men. [*Galatians 6:10*].

8. If there is no immediate need, should we give anyway? ——————————. [*Philippians 4:15-19*].

9. Does it glorify God when we give to the Church? —————————— [*Ephesians 3:21*].

V. SUBSTITUTE

1. Will God accept a substitute for what He has commanded? [*Matthew 15:9*]. Yes———————— No————————.

2. Do we have either examples or commands for the following methods of raising money to carry on the Lord's work?

Taxing?———————————————
Church suppers?————————————
Rummage sales?————————————
Pie suppers?——————————————

Shows?— — — — — — — — — — — — — —
Raffles?— — — — — — — — — — — — — — —
Entertainment?— — — — — — — — — — — -
Assessments?— — — — — — — — — — — —

3. Are we to have Bible authority for all things that we do? — — — — — — — — —. [*Colossians 3:17*].

4. Will the Lord's plan of giving take care of the Lord's work adequately? — — — — — — — — —. [*II Corinthians 9:8*].

5. Will God be pleased if we follow His plan only? — — — — — — — — — [*Revelation 22:14*].

Church Attendance

8

SCRIPTURE TEXT: "And let us consider one another to provoke unto love and good works; not forsaking our own assembling together, as the custom of some is, but exhorting one another; and so much the more, as ye see the day drawing nigh. For if we sin wilfully after that we have received the knowledge of the truth, there remaineth no more sacrifice for sins." [*Hebrews 10:24-26*].

INTRODUCTION

Our scripture text comes from the book of Hebrews which has many things to say relative to these Christian's spiritual condition. Instead of continuing steadfastly in the Apostles teaching, breaking of bread and prayer like the new Christians at Jerusalem, [*Acts 2:42*], they were neglecting their salvation. They were like the Israelites who had the Word preached to them but it did not profit them because of their lack of faith. [*Hebrews 4:2*]. They were not giving heed to what they had been taught. They had not grown spiritually. There were two indications of growth mentioned. One was to be able to tell right from wrong and the other was to be a teacher of others. [*Hebrews 5:11-14*]. While first principles serve a vital purpose, there is much more to the Christian life. They needed to go on unto perfection, but they had not. In fact, they were at the point of falling away. [*Hebrews 6:1-6*]. In chapter ten they were exhorted not to forsake the assembly. Verse 26 indicated that it is a sin to do so. Chapter twelve warns against the chastening of the Lord in order to bring about repentance.

There has always been work to do for the Lord's cause in obedience to Him since the Garden of Eden. Our first steps in faith must lead us on to develop our full potential for His cause. There is no more vital part of Christian development than church attendance. This should include every service, vacation Bible schools, gospel meetings, or other meetings when the congregation is urged to be present.

CHURCH ATTENDANCE

The Church Is The Lord's House	**I Tim. 3:15**
Christ Is The Head	**Col. 1:18; Eph. 1:22**
God Adds To The Church	**Acts 2:47; Col. 1:13**
Names Written In Heaven	**Heb. 12:23**
We Are His Children And His Servants	**Gal. 3:26, 27; II Tim. 2:24**

EXAMPLES AND COMMANDS	PURPOSE OF COMING TOGETHER	IT IS ESSENTIAL
Jerusalem Church [**Acts 2:42; 46**]	• To be taught .... [**Mt. 28:20; I Peter 2:2; Acts 20:28**]	• It will build you up .... [**Acts 20:32**]
Church at Troas [**Acts 20:7**]	• Observe The Lord's Supper .... [**I Cor. 11:23-26; Acts 20:7**]	• It will keep you from being led astray by false doctrines . [**Eph. 4:14**]
Corinthian Church [**I Cor. 16:2**]	• Sing .... [**Col. 3:16; Eph. 5:19**]	•It will help you grow to teach others. .... [**II Tim. 2:2; Heb. 5:12**]
Hebrew Christians [**Heb. 10:25, 26**]	• Give .... [**I Cor. 16:2; II Cor. 9:6,7**]	• It will make you feel a part of the family of God [**Rom. 12:5; 10:12-13; John 15:17**]
	• Pray .... [**Acts 2:42; II Thess. 5:17,18**]	• It will provide you with opportunities to work and serve. .... [**Mt. 25:14-30; John 15:1-8**]
	• Have Fellowship .... [**Acts 2:42**]	

T-208 CHRISTIAN LIGHTHOUSE, INC., P.O. BOX 159, MADISON, TENNESSEE 37115

FILL IN THE BLANKS

I. THE CHURCH IS A DIVINE PROVISION FOR MAN'S ULTIMATE SALVATION. [*MATTHEW 16:18*].

A. IT IS THE RESULT OF DIVINE SELECTION

1. What kingdoms did the devil offer Jesus if He would fall down and worship him? ———————————————————. [*Matthew 4:8, 9*].

2. Of what kind of a kingdom did the Jews want to make Jesus king? [*Acts 1:6*]. ———————————————————

3. Did the apostles think Jesus was going to establish a temporal kingdom here on earth? Yes ————— No —————.

4. What kingdom did He promise to establish? [*Matthew 16:18-19*].————————————————————

5. When was His kingdom established? ————————————————————————. [*Isaiah 2:23; Luke 24:44-49; Acts 2*].

6. Man has suggested substitutes for God's ways but are they right? Yes ——— No ———. [*Proverbs 14:12*].

B. THE CHURCH IS DIVINE IN ITS CONTENTS

1. "————— this ————— will ————————————church. [*Matthew 16:18*].

2. Who is the chief cornerstone? —————. [*Ephesians 2:20*].

3. Can we lay other foundations? Yes ——— No ———. [*I Corinthians 3:11*].

4. Christ is the ————— [*Ephesians 1:22*] and has all —————. [*Matthew 28:18*].

5. The Church is to wear whose name? —————. [*Ephesians 3:14-15; I Corinthians 1:10-13*].

6. Does the Church have a creed? Yes ——— No ——— and what is it centered around? —————. [*Matthew 16:16*].

C. THE CHURCH IS DIVINE IN IT'S LIFE

1. What is the Church in relationship to Christ? —————————. [*Ephesians 5:30*].

2. What is the divine guide of the Church? ——————————————. [*II Timothy 3:16-17*].

3. What are the divine conditions of entrance into His church? (1)————————— [*Romans 10:17*]; (2) ———————. [*Luke 13:3*]; (3) —————. [*Acts 8:37 and Matthew 10:32*]; (4) ———————. [*Matthew 16:16; Acts 2:38*].

D. THE CHURCH IS DIVINE IN IT'S OWNERSHIP

1. To whom does the Church belong? ——————————. [*Matthew 16:18*].

2. How was the Church purchased? [*Acts 20:28*].————

————————————————————————————————.

3. The Church and Christ are related as ————————

——————————————————. [*Ephesians 5:22-32*].

4. When will the Lord come to claim His Church?————

————————————. [*Matthew 24:36; Revelation 21:2*].

II. THE CHRISTIAN ASSEMBLY HAS A GOD GIVEN PLAN FOR WORSHIP.

A. TEACH:

1. The new Christians at Jerusalem continued steadfastly in

————————————— ——————————and ———————. [*Acts 2:42*].

2. Jesus said to teach, baptize and ————————————

——————————————————————[*Matthew 28:20*].

3. What does it mean to be steadfast as the Jerusalem

Christians were?——————————————————————

————————————————————————————————

B. PRAY: (See lesson on this subject).

1. The early Jerusalem Christians continued steadfastly in prayer. What are some things for which Christians should pray?

[*See Matthew 5:44; 6:11, 12; 9:38; 26:39, 41*].—————————

————————————————————————————————

————————————————————————————————

C. OBSERVE THE LORD'S SUPPER: (See lesson on this subject).

1. The breaking of bread referred to in Acts 2:42 is the

————————————————————————————————.

2. Early Christians came together at Troas to observe

————————————upon the ——————— day of the week. [*Acts 20:7*].

3. Why should the Lord's supper be so meaningful to a Christian?—————————————————————

—————————————————————————.

D. SING:

1. Early Christians were told to ——————— and make ——————————————in the —————————. [*Colossians 3:16; Ephesians 5:19*].

2. Is it possible for one to attend a worship service, and sing but not worship acceptably? [*John 4:4; I Corinthians 14:15*].

Yes ——————————— No ———————————.

3. What attitudes prompt one to sing praises to God, whether in public worship or at home? [*See Galatians 5:22, 23*].————

——————————————————————————

——————————————————————————.

4. What does it mean to sing with the spirit and the understanding? [*I Corinthians 14:15*].———————————

——————————————————————————.

5. Are there any examples in the early Church, or did the apostles ever authorize the use of any mechanical instrument in worship? Yes——————————————— No —————————.

E. GIVING: (See lesson on this subject.)

1. Paul told the Corinthians to give on the ———————— ———————————as God had ——————————— them. [*I* [*I Corinthians 16:2*].

2. Paul also taught, concerning giving, that he who ————————————bountifully will —————————— bountifully? [*II Corinthians 9:6, 7*].

3. Is it possible for a man to rob God? [*Malachi 3:8-10*].

Yes ————————————— No ———————————————.

III. CHRISTIAN FELOWSHIP AND THE REARING OF CHILDREN.

A. How often did the Jerusalem Christians meet? [*Acts 2: 46*].

——————————————————————.

B. The Church at Jerusalem continued steadfastly in fellowship. [*Acts 2:42*]. Why is Christian fellowship important?

——————————————————————

——————————————————————.

C. How does church attendance relate to training our children in the way they should go? [*Proverbs 22:6; Ephesians 6:1-4*]. ————————————————————

——————————————————————.

D. THERE IS A GRAVE DANGER IN NEGLECTING TO ASSEMBLE OURSELVES.

1. The exortation in Hebrews 10:25 is not ————————

of —————————————— together.

2. Does it say some do this very thing? Yes ———————

NO —————————.

3. If we do neglect willfully the assembly, have we

trodden under foot the ——————————————.[*Hebrews 2:9*].

E. THE ELDERS WATCH FOR OUR SOULS.

1. Who has God appointed as shepherds of His flock?

——————————————————————. [*Acts 20:17, 28*].

2. What should our attitude be toward them? ——————

——————————————————————. [*Hebrews 13:17*].

3. Who must they give an account to for our souls?

——————————————————————. [*Hebrews 13:17*].

4. Are all Christians to be "their brother's keeper?"

——————————————————————. [*Galatians 6:1*].

5. After all efforts have failed in getting a wayward and disorderly brother to repent, what is the Church to do? ————

————————————————————. *II Thessalonians 3:6*].

6. What is God's purpose in withdrawal of fellowship?

————————————————————. [*I Corinthians 5:5*].

7. What are some of the excuses people offer for not attending church services? [*See Matthew 22:1-6; Luke 14:16-24*].

————————————————————————————

————————————————————————————

————————————————————————————

————————————————————————————

The Indewelling Spirit

9

SCRIPTURE TEXT: "Jesus answered and said unto him, Verily, verily, I say unto thee, Except one be born anew, he cannot see the kingdom of God. Jesus answered, Verily, verily I say unto thee, Except one be born of water and the Spirit, he cannot enter the Kingdom of God. That which is born of the flesh is flesh; and that which is born of the Spirit is spirit. Marvel not that I said unto thee, Ye must be born anew, The wind bloweth where is will, and thou hearest the voice thereof, but knowest not whence it cometh, and whither it goeth: so is everyone that is born of the Spirit." [*John 3:3, 5-8*].

INTRODUCTION

The born again child of God gives evidence by his life that he is a converted person. It is possible for one to be baptized who has not truly repented, having submitted to baptism through wrong motives, Such a person has not been born of the water and the spirit. When Jesus gave the great commission, He said, ". . . All authority hath been given unto me in heaven and on earth. Go ye therefore, and make disciples of all nations, baptizing them into the name of the Father and of the Son and of the Holy Spirit: Teaching them to observe all things whatsoever I commanded you: and lo, I am with you always, even unto the end of the world." [*Matthew 28:18-20*]. When the gospel was preached for the first time, those who believed and whose hearts were pricked by Peter's message, asked what to do. "And Peter said unto them, Repent ye, and be baptized every one of you in the mane of Jesus Christ unto the remission of your sins; and ye shall receive the gift of the Holy Spirit." [*Acts 2:38*]. The word of God is an instrument of the Holy Spirit. When one obeys the gospel, he is given the indwelling spirit, "No man hath beheld God at any time: if we love one another, God abideth in us, and his love is perfected in us: hereby we know that we abide in him and he in us, because he hath given us of his Spirit. And we have beheld and bear witness that the Father hath sent the Son to be the Saviour of the world. Whosoever shall confess that Jesus is the Son of God, God abideth in him, and he is in God." [*I John 4:12-15*]. In Jesus' parable of the vine and the branches, He said, "I am the vine, ye are the branches: He that abideth in me, and I in him, the same beareth much fruit: for apart from me ye can do nothing. If a man abide not in me, he is cast forth as a branch, and is withered: and they gather them and cast them into the fire, and they are burned." [*John 15:5-6*]. Why cannot a man do anything if Christ does not dwell in him? Because man cannot overcome his carnal fleshly nature apart from God. "But I say, Walk by the Spirit, and ye shall not fulfil the lust of the flesh. For the flesh lusteth against the Spirit, and the Spirit against the flesh; for these are contrary the one to the other; that ye may not do the things that ye would." [*Galatians 5:16-17*]. Paul writes in the Roman letter, "For if ye live after the flesh, ye must die; but if by the Spirit ye put to death the deeds of the body, ye shall live." [*Romans 8:13-14*]. [*cf Galatians 4:6; Ephesians 4:30; 1:13; 5:18; II Corinthians 5:5; I Corinthians 1:22; Romans 8:23; II Timothy 1:14; Titus 3:5, 6; I Thessalonians 4:8; Acts 5:32; I John 3:24*]. The indwelling spirit is not a miraculous measure. We do not receive revelations. The word of God is our only guide. The chart will explain more in detail the work of the Holy Spirit in the past and present.

MEASURES OF THE SPIRIT

John 3:34

Baptismal	Secondary	Indewelling
TO	TO	TO
Apostles—Cornelius *Acts 2; Acts 10*	Some Disciples *Acts 8:12-18; 19:6*	All Christians *Acts 2:38, 5:32; Gal 4:6*
Christ—Administrator *Jno. 1:33; Matt. 3:11*	By Apostles *Rom. 1:11; Acts 8:18; 19:6*	When Baptized *Acts 2:38, 39; 5:32*
Not To Save *Acts 2:1-4; 11:13, 14; Mk. 16:16 I Peter 3:21*	Not To Save *Acts 8:12-18; 19:5, 6; Rom. 8:9; 1:11*	Dwells in Church *I Cor. 3:16; Eph. 2:20-22*
To Reveal Truth *Jno. 16:13, 14, 26; I Cor. 2:13*	Help 'til N.T. Written *Eph. 4:11-13*	Gives No Miracles *Rom. 8:9; 1:11; Jno. 10:41*
To Confirm Truth *Acts 1:8; 2:43; Mark 16:20; Heb. 2:3, 4; II Cor. 12:12*	Purpose of Gifts *I Cor. 12:1-10 NOT NEEDED NOW*	Not Spirit Baptized *Rom. 8:9; Eph. 4:5*
Ceased AD 64 *Eph. 4:5*	Ceased AD 96 *I Cor. 13:8-13*	Continues *Acts 2:38; 5:2*

SANCTIFICATION AND THE FRUIT OF THE SPIRIT

Garth Black, in his excellent book, *The Holy Spirit,* discusses sanctification and the fruit of the Spirit. He writes, "The New Testament teaches that the whole Christian life is to be one process of sanctification. Sanctification may be distinguished from conversion as growth is distinguished from birth. It is the perfecting of the saint, the bringing of the new born babe into the measure of the stature of the fullness of Christ. It is putting off the 'old man' and putting on the 'new man.' [*note Ephesians 4:22-24*].

"The babe in Christ is a new creature; old things have passed away and all things have become new. Now that he is in the family of God he must adjust to the new surroundings in the spiritual Kingdom and must grow and develop as a child of God. This growth and development, which is called sanctification, are works of the Holy Spirit which enables believers in Christ more and more to die to sin and live unto righteousness. Having been adopted into the family of God, Christian men and women are led by the Spirit of God in growth and development in the Christian life.

"The characteristic name of the Spirit in the New Testament is 'Holy', meaning separateness or apartness. The primary work of the Spirit in the life of the Christian is to make him holy or set him apart; to sanctify him.

"The ultimate aim of all the Spirit's work is to develop and perfect the Christian into the likeness of Christ. In a sense then all of the Spirit's work is included in the process of sanctification. All that the Spirit does Himself and through the instrumentality of the written word is looking toward the sanctification of the Christian until he attains a perfect holiness of character in the life to come.

"God through the Holy Spirit sanctifies as much of man's life as is absolutely yielded to him. He fills as much of the human heart as is opened to Him. So Christian growth consists of this; that as more and more of the heart is opened to God, the more the Christian can be sanctified. Sanctification cannot be forced upon an unyielding Christian.

"Although it is the duty and work of the Christian to perfect holiness in the fear of the Lord, it requires God's aid, received through the Holy Spirit.

"The Holy Spirit actually and powerfully assists the Christian in the struggle for eternal life. The Spirit is the author of all man's holiness, and in the struggle after victory over sin and temptation. He works in and with the Christian to bring about his sanctification.

"THE FRUIT OF THE SPIRIT"

"The result of the work of sanctification is called the fruit of the Spirit. [*Galatians 5:22 ff*]. Sanctification is growth and the holy life is fruit. When the Spirit leads a man there is movement and progress in his life as step after step he follows the Spirit's influence, each moment bringing him nearer to the goal. As the man is led by the Spirit he bears the fruit of the Spirit — a life filled with love, joy, peace and surrounded with an atmosphere of forebearance, kindness, goodness, honesty of purpose, ability to endure affront, and self-control. The Spirit bears fruit in every region of human life. All that fulfills the goal of life by bringing glory to God is of the Spirit.

"The chief work that the Holy Spirit has with Christians is to develop them into the likeness of Christ, to reproduce in them the beauty and glory of the personality of Christ. But one cannot develop into the likeness of Christ without bearing the fruit of the Holy Spirit. The test of the Christian life is whether it bears the fruit of the Spirit.

"In Galatians 5:22-23 the fruit of the Spirit is set forth by the Apostle Paul. [*Also note Romans 5:5; 14:17; 15:13; II Corinthians 6:6*]. 'But the fruit of the Spirit is love, joy, peace, longsuffering, kindness, goodness, faithfulness, meekness, self-control; against such there is no law.' In this passage the fruit of the Holy Spirit in the lives of faithful Christians is put in contrast with the works of the flesh. [*Galatians 5:19-21*]. It is as easy to recognize the fruit of the Spirit as it is to recognize the works of the flesh. [*Matthew 7:16-20*]. The Christian is characterized by his life in contrast to the life of those of the world. ''By their fruits ye shall know them.'' [*Matthew 7:16*]. All Christians are to bear the same kind of fruit; hence all Christians are to become like Christ. However, there are some who would profess to be Christians who quench the Holy Spirit, [*I Thessalonians 5:19*], or grieve the Spirit [*Ephesians 4:30*]. They refuse to be led by the Spirit and therefore cannot bear the fruit of the Spirit.

''It should be noted that the apostle Paul uses the singular in denoting the fruit of the Spirit. The nine attributes that he lists may thus be referred to as component parts of the 'fruit of the Spirit.' It cannot be said of anyone that he is truly bearing the fruit of the Spirit unless he is manifesting each characteristic which comprises that fruit. In other words, one must manifiest faithfulness and loving obedience to Christ as well as goodness, kindness, and patience. This is not to say that one must be bearing the fruit of the Spirit to the point of perfection before he can be described as bearing fruit, but he must be striving to that end. It should never be implied that an individual is a fruit-bearing Christian unless he is actively striving to demonstrate his love for the Lord by yielding his life in obedience to his will. [*John 14:15*].

''As the Christian grows in grace and in the knowledge of the truth of God day by day, he will bear the fruit of the Spirit. This growth and development, as witnessed in his life, is the process of sanctification being accomplished with the aid of the Holy Spirit.'' (Published by Biblical Research Press, 774 E. North 15th Street, Abilene, Texas 79601).

FILL IN THE BLANKS

I. THERE ARE THREE MEASURES OF THE HOLY SPIRIT AS HAS BEEN MANIFESTED BY THE BIBLE.

1. Spirit without measure was given to Christ only. [*John 3:34*].

   a. Baptismal measure. [*Acts 2 and Acts 10*].

   b. Secondary or laying on of hands. [*Acts 8:12-18; 19:6*].

   c. The indwelling measure given to all Christians. [*Acts 5:32*].

2. In order to receive the gift of the Holy Spirit, Peter said, ''—————————————— and be —————————.'' [*Acts 2:38-39*].

3. The baptismal measure was, or was not to save.

—————————— ——————————. [*Acts 2:1-4; 11:13-14*].

4. How many cases of Holy Spirit baptism are recorded in the New Testament? 2—— 4—— 6—— 10—— 20—— or 31——.

5. Who administers Holy Spirit baptism? any preacher Apostles ———————— or God ——————————.

6. How was the prophecy of Joel 2:28 fulfilled with only two cases of Holy Spirit baptism? ——————————————————.

7. The baptism of the Holy Spirit was to guide the Apostles into all —————————————— [*John 16:13; 14:26; I Corinthians 2:13*].

8. When we read the inspired word of God written by the Apostles, we have the same message they had. [*Ephesians 3:1-4*]. Yes —————— No ——————.

II. THE SECONDARY MEASURE, OR LAYING ON OF HANDS FOR THE PURPOSE OF bestowing a special gift to individuals was given to, all people ————————— some Christians ——————— or preachers only——————————————?

1. The gifts, such as, speaking with tongues, healing the sick, making the blind to see and etc., were given by, preachers, ————————————, apostles, ————————————, the Holy Spirit directly ———————————— or by certain evangelists ————————————————?

2. This gift was for the purpose of saving ———————, or helping to reveal God's will until the New Testament was written. Yes —————— No —————— [*Mark 16:15-20*].

3. This gift is needed now ——————————, not needed now ————————————?

4. The apostle Paul said this measure would pass away ————————————————————, or would not pass away

————————————? [*I Corinthians 13:8-13*].

III. THE INDWELLING MEASURE

1. This measure is given unto just a few ————————,

or all Christians —————————————? [*Acts 2:38*].

2. It is given with —————————, or without condition

————————————? [*Acts 2:38; 5:32*].

3. It will enable the one who receives it to speak in tongues and heal all manner of sickness. Yes ————————

No ————————————.

4. The condition upon which we receive the Holy Spirit is

faith only ————————— or obedience —————————? [*Acts 5:32*].

5. The obedience required includes faith and repentance

only ————————, or also includes baptism in water

———————————? [*Acts 5:32; 2:38*].

6. Through ——————————— we have access by the

————————————— unto the Father. [*Eph. 2:18-20*].

7. We must have the ———————— in order to have Christ. [*Romans 8:9*].

8. The ———————dwells in our hearts by faith. [*Ephesians 3:17*].

9. Christ dwells in our hearts by ————————————. [*Ephesians 3:17*].

10. God, Christ and the Holy Spirit all dwell in our hearts

by faith. Yes —————— No ——————. [*Ephesians 3:17; Romans 8:9-11*].

11. Our bodies are the —————————— of the Holy Spirit. [*I Corinthians 3:16:17*].

12. God will be displeased if we defile the temple. Yes

——————— No ————————?

13. We are to ——————— in our ———————— and our

————————— which are God's. [*Romans 8:13*].

14. The indwelling Spirit enables us to overcome. Yes ______ No ________?

15. What are the component parts of the "fruit of the Spirit?" [*Galatians 5:22-23*]. ____________________

____

16. Does the Spirit strengthen us as Christians? ______ [*Ephesians 3:16*].

17. The flesh is contrary to the Spirit. Yes ______ No ______ ? [*Galatians 5:17*].

18. Peace and edification are characteristic of the indwelling Spirit. Yes ______ No __________? [*Acts 9:31*].

The Second Coming of Christ

10

SCRIPTURE TEXT: "Watch therefore; for ye know not on what day your Lord cometh. But know this, that if the master of the house had known in what watch the thief was coming, he would have watched, and would not have suffered his house to be broken through." [*Matthew 24:42-44*].

INTRODUCTION

Moses, while being reared in fame and fortune, as the son of Pharoah's daughter, looked beyond this life. It is written of him, "By faith Moses, when he was grown up, refused to be called the son of Pharaoh's daughter; choosing rather to share ill treatment with the people of God, than to enjoy the pleasures of sin for a season." [*Hebrews 11:24-26*]. Moses was wise in that he could look to the end of all earthly matters, and thus make his decision to serve God. For us to fail to see the temporary nature of this life and judgement to come is to be blind and unable to see afar off. [*I Peter 1:9*].

Jesus illustrated man's duty and future judgment in three parables given in Matthew 25. (Read this chapter). The first one is about a wedding and the five wise and five foolish virgins who waited for the bridegroom to come. The wise carried extra oil for their lamps. The foolish carried no extra oil. While the bridegroom tarried they ran out of oil. While they went to buy oil the bridegroom came. The wise were ready and waiting and went in with him to the marriage and the door was shut. The foolish came and knocked and wanted in, but they were not permitted. The lesson from this parable is to always be prepared for the Lord's return. The Lord may come at any day or hour. "Watch therefore for ye know not the day nor the hour." [*Matthew 25:13*].

In the second story we have Christ depicted as a man who called unto him his servants and delivered unto them his goods. To one he gave one talent, to another two and to another five. Then he took his journey into a far country. He had placed them over his goods. Their opportunity and ability equalled their responsibility. [*Matthew 25:14-30*]. The man later returned and asked his servants for an accounting as to their stewardship. The servants with two and five talents had doubled theirs. The servant with one talent said he was afraid and did not increase the goods. This brought the master's condemnation. This illustrates how that Jesus has given us, His servants, charge over His work on this earth. All have been given opportunity and ability and thus have responsibility to carry out the work. The Lord will return! There will be a day of reckoning! Those who have served well will hear the welcome, ". . . Well done, good and faithful servant: thou hast been faithful over a few things, I will set thee over many things; enter thou into the joy of thy lord." [*Matthew 25:21*].

Those who have not served well will hear, "And cast ye out the unprofitable servant into the outer darkness: there shall be weeping and gnashing of teeth." This illustration teaches that God has given us all an opportunity to do His work and the responsibility to do it while we are upon this earth. He will return and we must give an account as to how we have discharged that responsibility.

In the third illustration, we have the judgement scene depicted: the Lord returning, all nations gathered before Him, and His separating them as a shepherd separates the sheep from the goats. The sheep had ministered to the hungry, thirsty, taken in the stranger, clothed the naked, visited the sick and those in prison. The only difference in what Christ said to those sheep on His right hand and the goats on His left hand was the little word "NOT". They did *not* do these things. But there was a vast difference in where they would be throughout eternity. He said, "And these shall go away into eternal punishment: but the righteous into eternal life." [*Matthew 25:46*].

We learn from this story the importance of being compassionate toward the needs of others. The sheep visit, serve and share, the goats do not.

THE SECOND COMING OF CHRIST

HOW?	WHEN?	WHERE?	WHY?

Literally as He went away	*Acts 1:11*
Every eye shall see Him	*Rev. 1:7*
At an unexpected time	*Matt. 24:44*
Suddenly as a thief	*I Thess. 5:2*
The earth will be burned up	*II Pet. 3:10*
Coming in fire taking vengeance	*II Thess. 1:7-9*
Living Saints will meet Him	*I Thess. 4:16*
Heralded by the trump of God	*I Thess. 4:16*
Bringing saints with Him	*Jude 14*
Coming to execute judgment	*Jude 14*
Resurrection of all	*I Cor. 15:50-58*
Death will be destroyed	*I Cor. 15:24-26*
Saints will be like Him	*I John 3:2*
Saints will be with Him	*I Thess. 4:17*
He will judge both living & dead	*II Tim. 4:1*
All Saints will be rewarded	*II Tim. 4:6-8; Jno. 5:28, 29*
Christ will deliver Kingdom to God	*I Cor. 15:24-26*

FILL IN THE BLANKS:

1. Would it be possible for Christ to be here and some not see Him? [*Revelation 1:7*]. ____________________

2. Is it probable that Jesus will come in a different manner than that in which He departed? [*Acts 1:11*]. ____________
____

3. Do you think men will know the exact time beforehand of His coming? [*Matthew 24:42*]. ____________________

4. Will His coming be prolonged so that everyone will have plenty of time to prepare after the first warning? [*I Thessalonians 5:2*]. ______________________________

5. Will this earth be restored to a pure state, and heaven be here on earth? [*II Peter 3:10*]. ____________________

6. Will the Lord come and bring peace and happiness to all mankind? [*II Thessalonians 1:7-9*]. ____________________

7. Will the Saints live with Him here upon the earth? [*I Thessalonians 4:16*]. ________________________

8. Will His coming be without sound? [*I Thessalonians 4:16*].

———————————————————————————

9. Will the Lord bring anyone with Him? [*Jude 14*]. ———————————————————————————

10. Is the Lord coming to establish a kingdom, or to execute judgment? [*Jude 15*]. ——————————————————

11. Will all be resurrected when He comes? [*I Corinthians 15-26*]. ——————————————————————————

12. What will the Lord do about death when He comes? [*I Corinthians 15:26*]. ——————————————————

13. Will the saints be like Jesus when He comes? [*I John 3:2*].

———————————————————————————

14. Will the saints be with Him? [*I Thessalonians 4:17*]. ——————————————————————————

15. According to the above, Christ is here now. Yes ————— No —————.

16. He will judge only the dead when He comes. Yes ———— No ——————. [*II Timothy 4:1*].

17. Only the apostles will get their reward when Christ comes again. True ——————————— False ———————————. [*II Timothy 4:6-8*].

18. Christ then will begin or end His reign; which? —————— [*I Corinthians 15:24-26*].

19. From the above Scriptures do you think Christ will establish a kingdom upon the earth and reign for a literal thousand years? Yes —————————— No ——————————.

11 The Church of Christ Is Scripturally Authentic

SCRIPTURE TEXT: "But the Spirit saith expressly, that in later times some shall fall away from the faith, giving heed to seducing spirits and doctrines of demons, through hypocrisy of men that speak lies, branded in their own conscience as with a hot iron; forbidding to marry, and commanding to abstain from meats, which God created to be received with thanksgiving by them that believe and know the truth." [*I Timothy 4:1-3*].

INTRODUCTION

The Church of Christ is neither Jewish, Catholic nor Protestant, but is as distinct from these religions as they are from each other. It claims no uninterrupted continuity back to the early days, but without arrogance or bigotry, the church of Christ *does* claim to be *scripturally identical* with the church which is revealed in the New Testament. You can test this claim, accurately and easily, and are requested to do so. You cannot afford to accept the bare word of anyone for so bold a claim, nor can you afford not to examine the grounds upon which it is made. You have too much at stake.

JESUS CHRIST ESTABLISHED ONE CHURCH

There has been but *ONE, SINLESS, DIVINE PERSON, JESUS CHRIST*. All others have sinned, and need to be saved by Christ (the only person who can save anyone), and identified with *His* church (the only *Divine* organization provided for the fellowship of those who *are* saved). No *other* person, therefore, has *any* authority to establish a church. For men (themselves sinners) to build other "churches" in competition with Christ's *divine* church is presumptions toward man's only Saviour, and is a sin against the credulity of their trusting followers. Let us face the facts. Just as God gave certain prophecies through whose fulfillments we were to recognize the Christ when He came, so likewise, He provided specific credentials by means of which men were to recognize and receive Christ's bride, His church, when she came into being. To fulfill these exacting Old Testament predictions, Christ's church was born into visible reality in the year 33 A.D., in Jerusalem, the specific city designated. Of the hundreds of churches which have come in existence through the centuries, only *one* church has met these divinely given requirements. You can read about *this* Church in complete and glorious detail on the pages of the New Testament. Modern "churches" may have many commendable features (many in fact, are aggressively promoting numerous Bible teachings), but it is an incontestable truth, nevertheless, that if they do not *meet* the *scriptural requirements as to founder, place and date, they are not the Church revealed in the Scriptures!* Thus compare any "church" point by point with the Bible's "blue-print" for Christ's Church. If it squarely meets *all* Bible requirements, it *is* the Bible church, but if it varies on any God-given teaching or practice, it is not the Bible church, simply because it is not the same, but is different from it. Just one exception ruins God's divine pattern, and Christ's "All authority" is replaced with the "authority" of him who makes the change. Thus a different "Lord" is accepted and obeyed, and Christ is dethroned. One degree off chartered course means shipwreck, and one point off from gospel truth is falsehood. Disobedience to God's Word brings damnation to the soul. A genuine $5.00 bill has the figure 392 cleverly worked into the shading of the bushes pictured on the reverse left side of the bill. Any addition or subtraction makes it undeniably a counterfeit, and makes it and the one using it liable to prosecution by the federal government. Is God less jealous for His eternal Church than Uncle Sam is for his money? Christ has but *one* bride, and every such "other woman" fradulently palming herself off as *His* bride, is condemned by every New Testament writer for spiritual adultery.

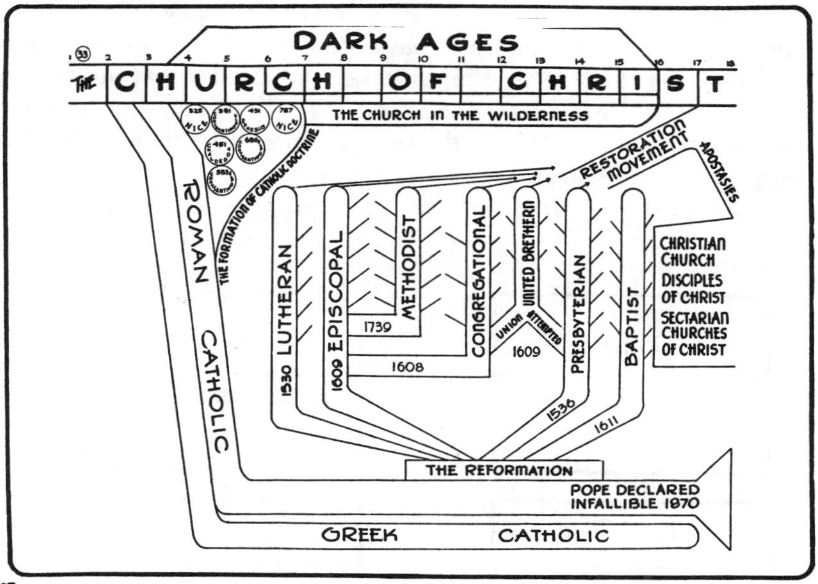

THE APOSTASY, REFORMATION AND RESTORATION OF THE NEW TESTAMENT CHURCH

The apostasy of the Church is foretold by the Lord. [*Acts 20:28-31; I Timothy 4:1-3; II Thessalonians 2:3-7*]. This began before the apostle John died. [*II John 9, 10*].

Some of the things in which the departure is seen:

The "clergy" and "laity" concept resulted in certain ones assuming power over others. Preachers soon took the place of elders and deacons. Bishops were appointed over them and a "Chief" bishop was over the bishops. Archbishops were appointed. Soon cardinals were appointed over archbishops. In the fifth century "John the Faster", who was a bishop, assumed the title "Bishop over all". However, this was bitterly contested. In the year 606 BONIFACE III was recognized by men, as the universal head of the church. (The Bible says Christ is the HEAD. *Ephesians 2:22, 23; Colossians 1:18*).

During the time these events were occuring, the Roman Government had favored the Church and was having much influence on it. Christianity suffered bitter persecution for a long time after the Church began. After the Apostles died, men began to change the government of the Church. In 325 A.D. the first human creed was written, the Nicene Creed. The Church had gained favor with the Roman Emperor, Constantine. He stopped the persecution of the Church. He appointed Christians to high offices and granted bishops of the Church judicial power. Even after Constantine's death the interplay between Christianity and the empire continued. This was one of the influences toward an ultimate development of a power structure similar to the Roman empire. Constantine was not baptized until just before his death. As Emperor he exercised great influence over church leaders. With the passing of years, the church government became almost identical in form to the old Roman Government as illustrated:

ROMAN CHURCH *ROMAN EMPIRE*

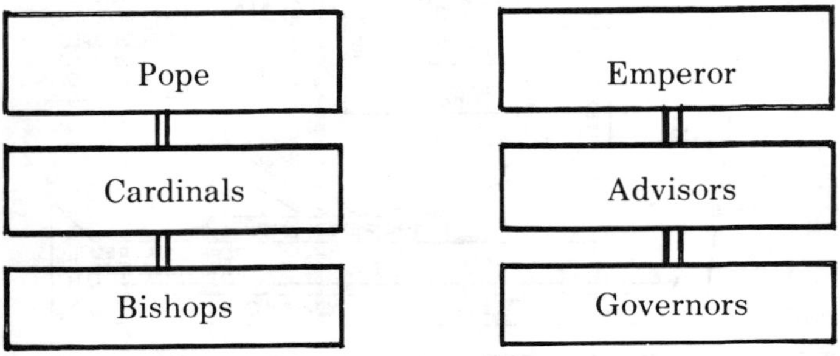

DEPARTURE IN DOCTRINE

HOLY WATER — A.D. 120 (after the Jewish cleansing).
PENANCE — For those who were excluded from the worship. They had special seats in the meeting and were required to undergo great humiliation and were seen as in need of prayer. (Thus the beginning of the mourner's bench).
THE NICENE CREED — 325 A.D. The first written "creed" except the Bible (Thus the beginning of creeds).
CELEBRATION OF MASS — Required to be in Latin, regardless of language spoken.
EXTREME UNCTION — 588 A.D. The dying annointed and prayed for. (the beginning of death-bed repentance "salvation").
INSTRUMENTAL MUSIC — 670 A.D. Introduced by Pope Vatalin.
PURGATORY — 593 A.D. Introduced by Gregory the Great. The priest would pray for the dead in order to redeem them from punishment or remorse. This required a fee from an interested party.
ELEVATION OF POPE — 709 A.D. Kissing Pope's big toe. Titles came into usage — "Reverend", "Father", etc.
TRANSUBSTANTIATION — 1000 A.D. Insisted that the bread and wine became the flesh and blood of Christ when properly "blessed" by a church official.
CELIBACY — 1015 A.D. Marriage forbidden among the clergy. Paul foretells this in I Timothy 4:1-3.
CHURCH AND STATE COMBINED — 728 A.D. (Pope wants all power).
CONFESSION — 1215 A.D. (confess to priest, receive forgiveness).
INDULGENCE — A "remission" of punishment still due after the guilt has been "forgiven" in the sacrament of penance.
SPRINKLING — 1311 A.D. At council of Ravenna. (Baptism non-essential).
BIBLE "CHAINED" — Given prayer book instead.
POPE DECLARED INFALLABLE — 1870 Pope Pius IX (535 bishops voted yes, two voted no) Man, not God, declared him infallable.

These are only a few of the things in which the church departed from the new Testament pattern.

The Scriptures teach us that such would happen in the last days. We can determine the Truth only by comparing present day teachings with the WORD OF GOD. We have the same word today that was in the beginning, therefore, we must have the same church.

THE REFORMATION MOVEMENT

JOHN WYCLIFFE. Wycliffe was one of the first to rebel against the Roman Catholic church in an attempt to reform it. He gave to the world a translation of the New Testament. Soon, all Europe was aroused with the thoughts of reforming the church.

MARTIN LUTHER. Luther opposed the sale of Indulgence and on October 31, 1517 he nailed to the door of Wittenberg Cathedral a parchment containing 95 theses or statements, nearly all relating to the sale of Indulgence. Luther was excommunicated from the Catholic church, and as a result the Confession of Faith. The Bible says, "There is one faith." [*Ephesians 4:5; Romans 10*]. He gave the world the doctrine of "Faith Only", [*James 2:24*].

ZWINGLI — Found 67 objections to Catholicism — was murdered 1530. (He said that all Christians should meet upon the first day of the week for communion).

JOHN CALVIN. A reformer who was driven from France in 1509 and gave the principles for the Presbyterian church in 1535 in Basil, Switzerland. (He gave the doctrine of predestination; election; total depravity; effectual calling of the Holy Spirit; impossibility of apostasy.)

HENRY VIII. Defied the authority of the Pope and started the church of England. It is catholic in doctrine and practice. It is a state church. The parliment makes its laws. It is known in America as the Episcopal.

JOHN SMITH. Started the Baptist church in Holland in 1606.

JOHN WESLEY. Wesley was an Episcopal priest. He was concerned with the lack of method and in 1729 broke with the Episcopal church and started the Methodist church.

In the beginning of the nineteenth century we find the religious world very much divided and confused. Sounds, noised dreams and visions were "proof" of religion and salvation. Creeds of men were in full force.

THE RESTORATION

JAMES O' KELLY. A Methodist in North Carolina, said, "From now on the name Christian only, and the Bible only."

THOMAS CAMPBELL. A Presbyterian in Pennsylvania started having communion every first day of the week for all the believers in the community, and declared: "From now on, the Bible only and the name Christian only."

ALEXANDER CAMPBELL. In Scotland he agreed with his father and came to America. (Motto was, "we speak where the Bible speaks and we are silent where the Bible is silent"). In the year 1824 in Lexington, Kentucky, a few men gathered together and agreed that they would go back to the Bible for name. [*Matthew 16:18; Romans 16:16; Acts 20:28; I Peter 4:16; Acts 11:26*]. They would teach nothing but the Bible for the plan of salvation. *Faith in God: Hebrews 11:6. Repentance: Acts 17:30, Confession: Romans 10:10; Acts 8:37. Baptism: Acts 2:38; Galatians 3:27; Romans 6:3-4;* would use only the Bible to direct their worship. *Singing: Colossians 3:16; Ephesians 5:19; I Corinthians 14:15. Prayer: I Timothy 2:8; Philippians 4:6. Contribution: I Corinthians 16:2; II Corinthians 9:6-7. Obedience is required: Hebrews 5:8-9; Revelation 22:14.*

FILL IN THE BLANKS

I. IDENTIFYING MARKS OF THE NEW TESTAMENT CHURCH

1. In what city did the New Testament Church begin? [*Isaiah 2:2, 3; Luke 24:47; Acts 2*]. ____________________

2. Were there several churches begun, each teaching different doctrines? Yes _______ No _______. How many churches were started? ________________ [*Matthew 16:18; Ephesians 1:22, 23; 4:4*].

3. Who is the founder of the Church? [*Matthew 16:18*]. ______________________________

4. What did people do to be saved? [*Mark 16:16; Acts 2:38; 8:26-39*]. ________________________

5. What kind of government did it have? [*I Timothy 3:1-13; Acts 20:16, 17*]. ________________________

6. Did the Apostles, preachers and teachers in the early church wear titles that would exalt one above the other? Yes _________ No _________.

7. What are some of the names used in reference to the New Testament church? [*Romans 16:16; I Corinthians 1:2; Ephesians 1:22, 23; 2:47*]. ____________________

____

8. What is God's attitude toward religious division? [*John 17:20, 21; I Corinthians 1:10-13*]. ________________

____

9. When we obey the same gospel as taught by the Apostles, what kind of Christians will we be? ____________

____

10. When we follow the Apostolic pattern for the Church today, are we restoring the New Testament pattern of the Church? Yes __________ No __________.

12 Finding My Place In The Church

SCRIPTURE TEXT: "Wherefore my beloved brethren, be ye steadfast, unmovable, always abounding in the work of the Lord, forasmuch as ye know that your labor is not vain in the Lord." [*I Corinthians 15:58*].

INTRODUCTION

Finding our place in the work of the Church does not limit our activities to the church building. There are many good works in which everyone can engage. The chart describes many of these. When we think of the work of the Church, we must ask, "What is the mission of the Church?" Jesus told why He came when He said, "For the Son of man came to seek and to save that which was lost." [*Luke 19:10*]. While Jesus was with His disciples He said, ". . . as the Father hath sent me, even so send I you." [*John 20:21*]. Therefore, the primary task of the Church is to take the good news of Christ to the lost world. If the elders have not asked you to do anything, then talk with them about what you feel you can do and let them know of your desire to be used. Do not wait for someone to give you a job before you go to work, remember that Christ gave you the job of winning lost souls to Him. You have friends who are not Christians, begin to work toward winning them to Christ. Read the book, *Introduction To Soul Winning,* edited by Clayton Pepper. Perhaps, your class might desire to study this after this quarter's lessons. A simple method for soul winning will be given later in this lesson.

All of us understand what it means to labor, toil and work in the secular realm. We also understand that if there is no work, there is no pay. Many in the realm of religion expect a reward when they have not used their talents or borne fruit. The one talent man was lost because he did not use his talent.[*Matthew 25:14:30*]. The branch that bears fruit is purged, so that it can bear more fruit. But the branch that does not bear fruit, is cut off and cast into the fire. [*John 15:1-10*]. Christian fruitfulness is necessary. However, it is still by the grace of God that we are saved.

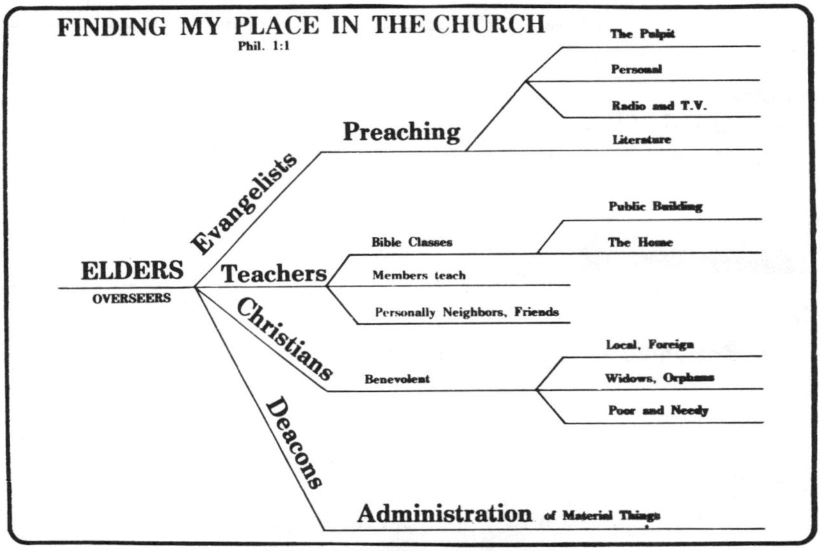

FILL IN THE BLANKS

I. GOD EXPECTS EVERYONE TO WORK AND THERE IS A PLACE FOR HIM.

1. Jesus taught a lesson in Matthew 25:14-30 concerning our_ _.

2. Did the early church recognize their stewardship? Yes _ _ _ _ _ _ _ _ _ No _ _ _ _ _ _ _ _ _ _. [*Acts 5:42; 8:4; 4:34, 35*].

3. To whom do we actually belong? [*I Corinthians 6:20*].

_ _

II. THE OVERSIGHT OF THE CHURCH.

1. Who is to have the oversight of the local church? [*I Peter 5:2*]. _

2. Does God's plan call for elders in every congregation?

_ _[*Acts 14:23*].

3. Over how many congregations is one set of elders to rule? ——————————————————————

4. Is it the Lord's plan that I, as a member, submit to the elders? [*Hebrews 13:17*]. ———————————————

5. Who is responsible for carrying out the "Great Commission"? elders, ——————— deacons, ———————, evangelists, —————————, the Church —————————? [*Ephesians 3:10*].

6. Who is to do the work of an evangelist? [*II Timothy 4:2; Hebrews 5:12-14*]. ——————————————————

7. How may he do this? —————————————————— [*Acts 8:26-39*].

8. To whom is the teacher responsible? ————————— and —————————— ——————————————.

9. Can one be a teacher and not teach publicly? —————— [*Acts 5:42*].

10. What opportunities are there for the teacher to teach? [*Luke 19:1-10; John 1:40-45*]. ——————————————————

11. Who needs teaching? [*Mark 16:15, 16*]. ——————————

12. Must our help be confined to those who are members of the Church? [*Galatians 6:10*]. ——————————————————

13. In what way can deacons serve? [*Acts 6:1-6*]. —————— ——————————————————————————————————

What else did Stephen and Philip do? [*Acts 7 & 8*]. ————————————————————————————

14. May a deacon also preach and teach? [*Acts 8:5*]. ——————————————————————————————————

15. Are all Christians responsible to teach others? [*I Timothy 2:2; Hebrews 5:12-14*]. Yes ——————— No ———————.

A METHOD THAT YOU CAN USE TO WIN OTHERS TO CHRIST

In recent years a marked King James Version of the New Testament entitled "Way of Salvation New Testament" was published for soul winning. In the lower right front cover are the words "You Can Learn The Way Of Salvation In Less Than 10 Minutes!! Please turn to page 256." This began a chain reference of scriptures, all underlined in red. This Bible was designed as a teaching tool for you to use, explaining the verses to the prospect. Also, five charts were included relating to salvation and the Church. This one lesson offers perhaps the simplest systematic approach available for teaching the lost.

This Bible is now out of print. Mark your own Bible putting 1 Corinthians 15:1-4 in the front of it. Put the next reference at the bottom of that page and the page number where it is found in your Bible. Do this on all references. You will have a fine chain reference for teaching.

THE MESSAGE AND THE METHOD

How do you begin discussing one's need for Christ? Let love guide you as you make a tactful approach. It is not necessary to offend. Here is a simple approach that has been used: "Mr. Jones, do you know that if you died today that you would go to heaven?" "No sir." "It is wonderful to know. Did you ever think that you would like to know that if you died you would go to heaven?" "Yes sir." "Let me ask you a question: Do you feel that if I could show you in the Bible exactly how you could know, and if you could understand it, would you be willing to do it?"

As you read these scriptures, discuss how you would explain them to the person whom you might be teaching.

PAUL EXPLAINS WHAT THE GOSPEL IS: "Moreover, brethren, I declare unto you the gospel which I preached unto you, which also ye have received, and wherein ye stand: by which also ye are saved, if ye keep in memory what I preached unto you, unless ye have believed in vain. For I delivered unto you first of all that which I also received, how that Christ died for our sins according to the scriptures." [*I Corinthians 15:1-4*].

ALL HAVE SINNED: "For all have sinned, and come short of the glory of God." [*Romans 3:23*].

SIN PAYS WAGES: "For the wages of sin is death; but the gift of God is eternal life through Jesus Christ our Lord." [*Romans 6:23*] [*cf Rev. 21:8*].

CHRIST TOOK THE PENALTY OF OUR SINS UPON HIM: "For when we were yet without strength, in due time Christ died for the ungodly . . . But God commendeth his love toward us, in that, while we were yet sinners, Christ died for us.'' [*Romans 5:6, 8; cf Isaiah 53:3-7*].

THE GOSPEL IS:

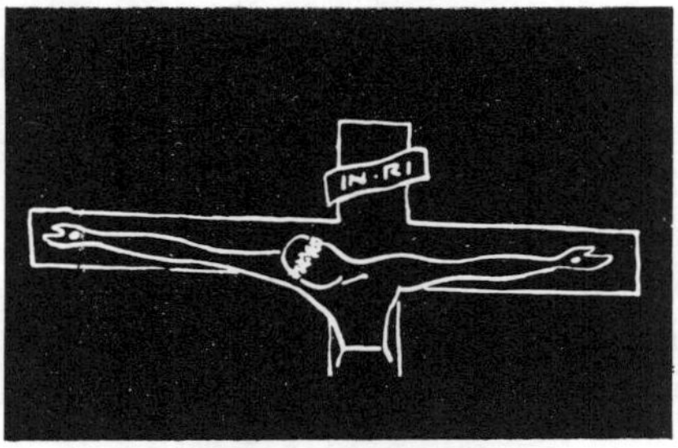

THE DEATH

BURIAL

AND RESURRECTION

JESUS SAID GO PREACH THE GOSPEL TO EVERY CREATURE: ''And he said unto them, Go ye into all the world, and preach the gospel to every creature. He that believeth and is baptized shall be saved: but he that believeth not shall be damned.'' [*Mark 16:15-16*].

HOW DOES ONE OBEY THE GOSPEL? ''Know ye not, that so many of us as were baptized into Jesus Christ were baptized into his death. Therefore, we are buried with him by baptism into death: that like as Christ was raised up from the dead by the glory of the father, even so we also should walk in newness of life. For if we have been planted together in the likeness of his death, we shall be also in the likeness of his resurrection: Knowing this, that our old man is crucified with him, that the body of sin might be destroyed, that henceforth we should not serve sin, For he that is dead is freed from sin.'' [*Romans 6:3-7*].

One dies to sin through repentance

One is buried in baptism

One rises to walk in newness of life.

THOSE WHO HAVE OBEYED THE GOSPEL HAVE BEEN MADE FREE FROM SIN: "But God be thanked, that ye were the servants of sin, but ye have obeyed from the heart that form of doctrine which was delivered you. Being made free from sin, ye became the servants of righteousness." [*Romans 6:17-18*].

THE GOSPEL WAS PREACHED ON PENTECOST AND LOST MEN WERE TOLD WHAT TO DO TO BE SAVED: "Now when they heard this, they were pricked in their heart, and said unto Peter and to the rest of the apostles. Men and brethren, what shall we do? Then Peter said unto them, Repent, and be baptized every one of you in the name of Jesus Christ for the remission of sins, and ye shall receive the gift of the Holy Ghost. For the promise is unto you, and to your children, and to all that are afar off, even as many as the Lord our God shall call." [*Acts 2:37-39*].

THOSE WHO DO NOT OBEY THE GOSPEL WILL BE LOST: "And to you who are troubled rest with us, when the Lord Jesus shall be revealed from heaven with his mighty angels. In flaming fire taking vengeance on them that know not God, and that obey not the gospel of our Lord Jesus Christ: Who shall be punished with everlasting destruction from the presence of the Lord, and from the glory of his power." [*II Thessalonians 1:7-9*].

CHRIST IS THE AUTHOR OF ETERNAL SALVATION TO ALL WHO OBEY HIM: "Though he were a Son, yet learned he obedience by the things which he suffered: and being made perfect, he became the author of eternal salvation unto all them that obey him;" [*Hebrews 5:8, 9*].

MAN DOES HAVE A PART IN HIS SALVATION: "Ye see then how that by works a man is justified, and not by faith only." [*James 2:24*].

THOSE WHO ARE BLESSED ARE THOSE WHO DO THE LORD'S COMMANDMENTS: "Blessed are they that do his commandments, that they may have a right to the tree of life, and enter in through the gates into the city." [*Revelation 22:14*].

EXAMPLES OF CONVERSION

The "Way of Salvation New Testament" has a portion of the book of Acts included in the back. This includes the following cases of conversion: The Pentecostians, Acts 2:37-47; The Samaritians, Acts 8:12, 13; The Ethiopian Nobleman, Acts 8:27-40; Captain Cornelius, Acts 10:1-48; A Merchant Named Lydia, Acts 16:14, 15; The Philippian Jailor, Acts 16:30-34; Crispus of Corinth, Acts 18:7, 8; Saul of Tarsus, Acts 22:6-16. The following charts are included in the back of the Bible for further study.

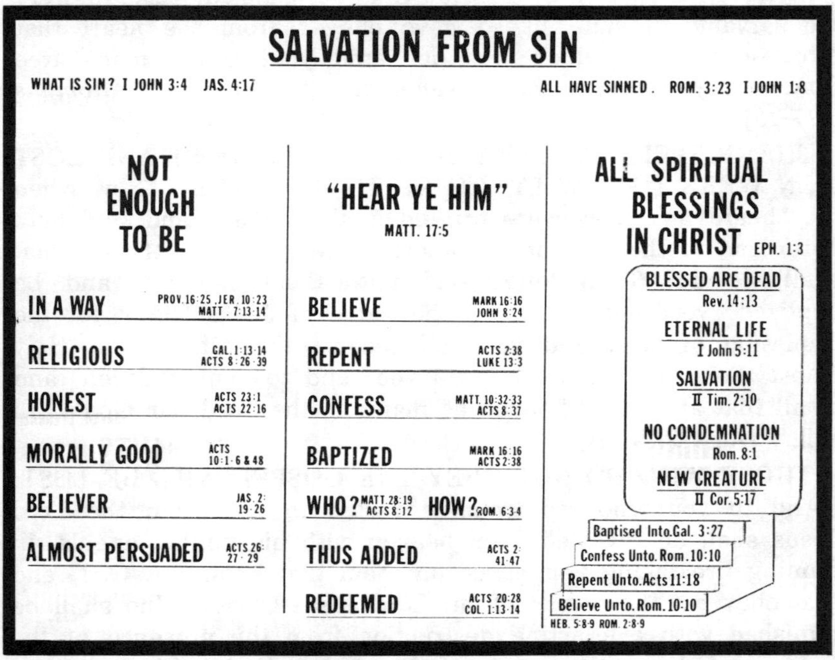

"SEARCH THE SCRIPTURES" (John 5:39 & Acts 17:11)

INSTRUCTIONS: Draw a line from the case of conversion to what the BIBLE says they did. Then draw a line from "YOU" to what you did to be saved.

JEWS (Acts 2:36-41)	page 173 •	• HEARD
SAMARITANS (Acts 8:5, 12)	page 183 •	• BELIEVED
SIMON (Acts 8:13)	page 183 •	• REPENTED
EUNUCH (Acts 8:26-39)	page 184 •	• CONFESSES CHRIST
SAUL (Acts 9:3-18; 22:16)	page 185 •	• WERE BAPTIZED
CORNELIUS (Acts 10:1-48)	page 187 •	• SAVED BY FAITH ONLY
LYDIA (Acts 16:13-16)	page 198 •	• "GOT RELIGION"
JAILER (Acts 16:25-34)	page 199 •	• PRAYED THROUGH
CRISPUS (Acts 18:8)	page 202 •	• JOINED DENOMINATION
	Y O U •	• ACCEPTED CHRIST

DOES THE ACCOUNT OF YOUR CONVERSION COMPARE COMPLETELY WITH WHAT THE BIBLE DEMANDED OF THESE PEOPLE? (Read Romans 8:16 also Jeremiah 10:23 and Prov. 14:12)

AFTER CONVERSION

ACTS 2:38
ACTS 22:16
SAVED - PAST SINS

THINGS TO REMEMBER

NEW CREATURE	II COR. 5:17 ROM. 6:4
BABES IN CHRIST	I PET. 2:2 I COR. 3:1-2
CRITICAL PERIOD	MATT. 4:1-11 I COR. 10:11-13
POSSIBILITY OF FALLING	JOHN 8:31 I JOHN 2:1-2, ACTS 8:17-24
REPRESENTATIVE	II COR. 3:2 I TIM. 4:12
CHRIST YOUR EXAMPLE	HEB. 12:1-2 I COR. 3:1-7

I TIM. 4:16
REV. 2:10
SAVED ETERNALLY

GOD WANTS YOU TO

LOVE HIM FIRST	MATT. 22:37 MATT. 10:37
STUDY	II TIM. 2:15 ACTS 17:11
PRAY	PHIL. 4:6-7 I TIM. 2:8
ASSEMBLE	HEB. 10:25-27 MATT. 18:20
GIVE	I COR. 16:1-2 II COR. 9:6-7
HELP SAVE OTHERS	MATT. 28:19-20 JOHN 15:1-6 & 16

THE NEW TESTAMENT CHURCH

Founder Christ	Where Jerusalem	When AD 33	Head Christ
MATT. 16:18	ISA. 2:3 ACTS 2:5,47	ACTS 2:	EPH. 1:22

ORGANIZATION PHIL. 1:1	Elders	Tit. 1:5-7, I Pet. 5:1-3, Acts 20:28, I Tim. 3:1-7
	Deacons	Acts 6:1-6, I Tim. 3:8-13
	Members	Acts 2:41-47, Col. 1:13, I Cor. 1:2
NAME EPH. 3:15	Church of God	I Cor. 1:2, Acts 20:28
	The Body of Christ	Col. 1:18, Eph. 1:22-23
	Churches of Christ	Matt. 16:18, Rom. 16:16
	Bride of Christ	Rom. 7:4, Rev. 21:9
NAME EPH. 3:15	Disciples	John 15:8, Acts 11:26
	Saints	Rom. 1:7, I Cor. 1:2, Phil. 1:1
	Brethren	Luke 8:21, Gal. 6:1
	Children	Gal. 3:26, I John 2:1
	Christians	Acts 11:26, 26:28, I Pet. 4:16
CREED	Jesus Christ	Matt. 16:16-18, 10:32-33-Acts 8:37
RULE OF FAITH & PRACTICE	Word of God	Matt. 28:18-20, II Tim. 3:16-17, II Pet. 1:3, Jas. 1:21
WORSHIP	Sing	Col. 3:16-Eph. 5:19, I Cor. 14:15, Heb. 2:12
	Pray	I Thes. 5:17
	Teach	Acts 5:42
	Communion	Acts 20:7, I Cor. 11:23
	Contribution	I Cor. 16:1-2
MISSION	Save Souls	Matt. 5:13-16, John 15:8, 16, I Tim. 4:16, II Tim. 2:2, Heb. 5:12
WARNING	Be Faithful	Matt. 15:9-Matt. 15:13, Gal. 1:6-8, II John 9: , Rev. 22:18-19

CONCLUSION

After presenting the lesson, ask the prospect if he understands, if so ask him to become a Christian now. If he does not understand teach him further, then read the story of the conversion of the nobleman in Acts 8:26-39 and ask him if he knows as much as this man did. If so, ask him to make the decision now that this Ethiopian made.

Going On Unto Perfection

13

SCRIPTURE TEXT: "Wherefore leaving the doctrine of the first principles of Christ, let us press on unto perfection; not laying again a foundation of repentance from dead works, and of faith toward God." [*Hebrews 6:1*].

INTRODUCTION

Hebrews 6:1 and 2, tell us that we should go on toward perfection and if we do not there is a danger of laying again a foundation of dead works after becoming a Christian. When this happens, it must be repented of, and a return must be made to our first love. [*Revelation 2:4, 5*]. While first principles are vital to our coming to Christ, there is much beyond this to be achieved. The early Christians were exhorted to leave the things that a babe in Christ would need and move onward toward perfection. Baby food is important in the life of a baby, as one grows it is necessary to discontinue this type of food. Paul saw a high calling in Christ and he pressed toward it. He said, "Brethren, I count not myself yet to have laid hold: but one thing I do, forgetting the things which are behind, and stretching forward to the things which are before." [*Philippians 3:13, 14*].

The Hebrew writer gave two indications of spiritual growth in chapter five, verses twelve through fourteen. One was, ". . . when by reason of the time ye ought to be teachers . . ." and the second one was being able to ". . . discern good and evil." Just before Jesus ascended to Heaven He gathered the Apostles around Him and said, "Go ye into all the world, and preach the gospel to the whole creation." (Mark 16:15). Today, the gospel is in earthen vessels, we who are Christians. [*II Corinthians 4:7*]. The eternal destiny of souls is in our hands, and our destiny rests upon whether we carry out this responsibility. [*Ezekiel 3:17, 28*].

Spiritual growth will enable us to teach others. This does not mean that it takes a long time. For we can even now begin teaching others what we know and win others to Christ.

The second indication of growth is being able to know right from wrong. Parents expect children to know much about right and wrong by the time they are ten or twelve years of age. There are many worldly things that one must "give up." [*Matthew 16:24-26*]. Some things that indicate spiritual weakness are swearing, immodest dress, drinking, smoking, going to worldly social settings and entertainment. Perhaps, you can name others.

The Apostle Peter gave a list of seven things, stating that those who do these things shall never fall. [*II Peter 1:5-11*]. It is therefore important that we have a full understanding of these things.

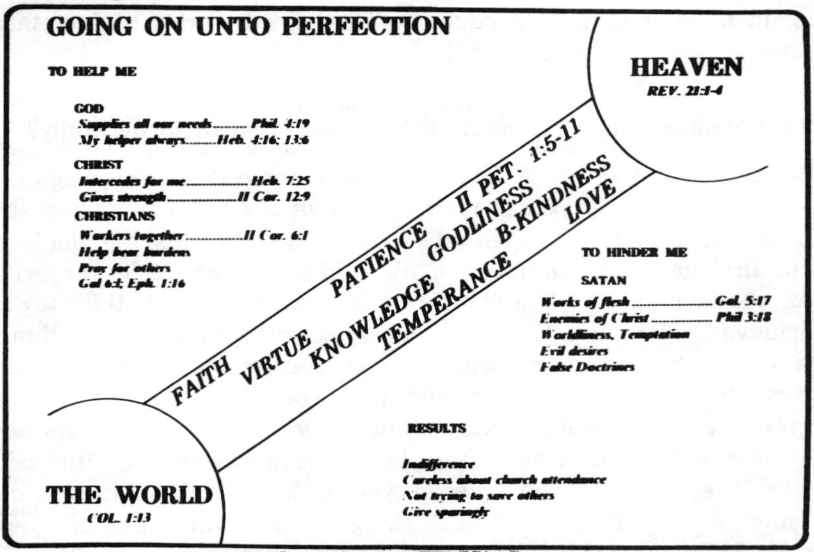

FILL IN THE BLANKS

1. Will the faith that led us to obey the gospel save, if we do not add to this faith? Yes __________ No __________.

2. Virtue is moral courage to stand for the right. How did Abraham and Daniel show moral courage? [*Hebrews 11:8; 11:17; Daniel 6*]. ______________________________

____

3. List several reasons for adding knowledge to our faith. [*Matthew 28:18-20; I Peter 3:15; Philippians 1:16; John 12:48; Psalm 119:105; James 1:23; Revelation 20:12; Matthew 4:1-11; II Timothy 2:15*]. ______________________________

____

____

4. Temperance means self control. In what ways do we need self control? [*James 1:19, 20:26; 3:5, 6; I Timothy 6:10; I Thessalonians 5:22; I Corinthians 9:27*]. _____________

____

____

5. What are some of the ways in which we need to exercise patience? [*Hebrews 10:36; 12:1; Romans 2:7; I Thessalonians 5:14; Luke 21:19*]. ______________________

____

____

6. Just being religious is not enough, we must put on "God-likeness" or Godliness. What does it mean to be godly?

[*II Peter 1:3-4; Titus 1:11-12*]. ____________________

____

7. What is brotherly kindness? [*I John 3:15-17; Ephesians 4:32; Luke 10:27; Galatians 6:10; Luke 10:27*]. __________

____

____

8. Why is love so powerful and important? Define the meaning of love and tell what it can do? [*I Corinthians 13; Colossians 4:13; I John 4:8, 16; John 3:16; Romans 5:8; I John 4:19; Matthew 22:36-38*]. ____________________

____

____

9. In what will those who do these things not be lacking? [*II Peter 1:8*]. ________________________

____

10. What is the condition of the person who does not add these Christian graces? [*II Peter 1:9*]. _______________

____

11. What does it mean to "Go on unto perfection?" [*Hebrews 6:1*]. ______________________________

____

OTHER BOOKS FROM QUALITY PUBLICATIONS

First Principles

Gary and Marylyn Underwood. **Don't lose your new converts. When you lead a soul to Christ, help keep him faithful to Christ by using this effective Bible study material.**

You Can Trust Your Bible

Neale Pryor. **An excellent study demonstrating the Bible as the perfect Word of God.**

Expanding Outlines Of the New Testament

Harvey Childress. **A proven method of teaching/learning the New Testament.**